Mundi is a series co
international essay

Titles include:

Essays on the Scottish Enlightenment   George Davie
Jan Lobel from Warsaw   Luise Rinser
Essays   Elsa Morante

The Scottish Enlightenment
and Other Essays

The Scottish Enlightenment

and Other Essays

George E. Davie D. Litt., FRSE

With a foreword by James Kelman

Polygon
EDINBURGH

© George Davie 1991

Polygon
22 George Square, Edinburgh

Set in Sabon
by Koinonia, Bury and
printed and bound in Great Britain
by Redwood Press, Melksham, Wiltshire

British Library Cataloguing in
    Publication Data
Davie, George E. (George Elder)
    Essays on Scottish enlightenment.
    1. Scottish philosophy
    I. Title
    192

ISBN 0-7486-6069-0

Contents

Acknowledgements

The author and publisher wish to thank The Historical Association for permission to print *The Scottish Enlightenment* (1981); Dundee University for permission to print *The Social Significance of the Scottish Philosophy of Common Sense* (1972); Scottish Academic Press for permission to print a version of *The Making of the Shorter Ferrier* (1985); and *Edinburgh Review* for permission to print *Scottish Philosophy and Robertson Smith* (1985). Particular thanks are due to James Kelman for his foreword.

Foreword

As well as offering an introduction to the intellectual struggles in Scotland during the 18th and 19th centuries, these essays by George Davie allow an insight into some of the more crucial issues in modern times. The sorts of questions then being raised were brought about by the need to push the country forwards in line with contemporary development in other parts of Europe, and derive from the primary problem of how to reconcile economic expansion with the moral vitality of the populace. These questions are philosophical as well as political. But in one way or another most people reflect upon them: in fact, they are part of our common attempt to examine and make sense of the basic principles that govern our existence as human beings.

Do people have the fundamental right to freedom? By what authority does one person, or group of people, control another? Is there a case for assuming responsibility over the social and spiritual life of other adults? When does 'teaching' become colonization? Can one culture ever be 'better' than another? Is the attempt to deny your right to exploit me 'unconstitutional'?

Davie assembles a coherent picture of a continuous intellectual movement in Scotland, a genuinely democratic movement. But the ultimate challenge of his work seems to me to lie in the context he sets this picture, which is theory of knowledge, the study now known as 'epistemology', a term first coined by the

Scottish philosopher and poet James F. Ferrier. Davie's work is of major significance and it is vital the public at large are given access to it. The four essays comprising this short book provide the introduction to that.

James Kelman
Glasgow
1990

The Scottish Enlightenment

Church and State
Fletcher's Philosophical Politics
Scepticism
The Student Societies
David Hume, Thomas Reid, Adam Smith
The Argument with Andrew Fletcher
The Problem of Scottish Reform

Church and State

The seventeenth century, after an uncertain start, suddenly seemed in its last decade to herald a new dawn in the affairs of Scotland. The Scots were elated by the unexpected but all the more welcome effect of the Glorious Revolution in freeing both their State and their Church from a century of remote control operated from London by the monarch they shared with England. They were intoxicated, even, by the opportunity thus belatedly offered of realising their long-deferred reformation ideal of a constitution finely balanced as between church and state: a constitution by which they would govern themselves through the cooperation of a pair of mutually critical but mutually complementary assemblies, the one concerned with politics and law, the other with the distinguishable, but nevertheless inseparable sphere of ethics and of faith. The ascendant presbyterians began to dream of redressing the balance, in the spiritual field as well as in the temporal, between themselves and their fellow presbyterians the Dutch – whose fortunes both in culture and in commerce the Lord, for His inscrutable purposes, had hitherto favoured, as they thought, somewhat excessively as compared with their own more deserving situation. In the sphere of the spirit, these presbyterians were determined to restore to its pristine splendour 'the famed learning of the nation' by instituting a systematic reform of their universities, to be remodelled on the Dutch example

1

and financed out of the revenues of the bishoprics abolished by the Revolution.[1] In the kingdom of the flesh, they would promote the economic growth of their extremely retarded country by founding colonial settlements beginning with the advantageously situated Isthmus of Darien.

In the academic sphere, the dominant presbyterians opened the doors of their universities to larger numbers of less well-off students by instituting bursaries for those who felt a stirring of the spirit. At the same time they set about monitoring the intellectual standards by instituting an interlocking set of committees from both inside and outside the universities, convened with regularity and efficiency as surviving minutes show, for the purpose of criticising and sanctioning draft courses in logic, in ethics, in physics, in pneumatology and in rhetoric. It was hoped that these courses, produced by the regents of the various universities with a remuneration of £50 apiece, would not only furnish textbooks more suitable to the needs of Scottish students than the continental and English manuals currently in use in the country, but might even make a favourable impression furth of Scotland, both by the quality of their presentation and the critical moderation of their discussion. Starting a little later in the decade, the Company of Scotland recruited colonists, hired the ships and prepared the Darien expedition. It seemed as if Scotland would at last make the grade in the world of commerce and the world of culture, and be able to take her due place among the nations of the West. But before the decade was out, the spectacular successes expected from both ventures had turned into a couple of spectacular failures which rudely awakened the Scots from their optimistic daydreams.

The failure of the Darien scheme gave rise to an argument among the Scots about political economy: an argument as to whether Scotland's economic salvation depended, as William Paterson argued, on a union which would ensure free trade with England and her colonies, or could be achieved without loss of independence, either by John Law's scheme of credit control or by Andrew Fletcher's more drastic ideas for a development based on forced labour and Highland clearances. Soon, however, the debate reached its critical point when it became clear that the English offer of free trade which the Scots wanted was depen-dent on them accepting an incorporation of their parliament in that of England, which in effect would confirm English ideas as to the provincial and sub-ordinate status of Scotland's legislature and make nonsense of the Scottish claims as to the sovereign status of their nation. Unable in the circumstances to achieve the federal union which in the Scottish view might reconcile material expediency with the principle of parity as a nation, the Scots cut the knot by making one of those distinctions of a metaphysical sort of which they were so fond and of which the English were so suspicious; that is to say, they sought to have it both ways by consenting, in a practical sense, to abolish their parliamentary independence for all time in the interests of economic advantage, while simultaneously in order to keep their consciences right in the matter of first principles, they refused to vote their parliament out of existence at its final meeting, simply proroguing it *sine die*. They thus allowed the debate to continue on an intellectual plane, and enabled Frances Hutcheson to argue, in post-1730 Glasgow, that the Union was defective in failing to provide Scotland with institutional machinery for defending its rights as a nation.

Fletcher's Philosophical Politics

The Scottish Enlightenment is here understood as the Scottish success in assimilating and developing the brilliant ideas which had first come to light among the English (in a fit of absence of mind) during the days of Locke and Newton only to be neglected in the era of Walpole, when the metaphysical complications of its intellectual discoveries began to show themselves. To understand better how these parallel debates about Scottish freedom in the temporal and in the spiritual sense prepared the way for this Enlightenment, it is important to study how these twin currents of Scottish argumentation, concerned with faith and morals, and with politics and law, began to clash and fuse with one another.

Andrew Fletcher's idea of a national politics was to make the case for Scotland's self-government irrefutable by basing it not on the pragmatic considerations which generally weigh with countries in these matters, and more particularly with the sister nation, but by arguing things out systematically, by a sort of appeal to first and fundamental principles. The country's economic development was, Fletcher conceded, the essential task for Scots of his age, but this growth could not be promoted by consenting to a union which involved the country being governed by remote control as a province of a great nation six times its size, and represented by parliamentarians who, to take their seats, had to go to the great metropolis situated furth of Scotland. Disapproving of great cities as seats of government, Fletcher described the anonymity, the alienation, the narrow professionalism and the luxuriousness inseparable from the metropolitan way of life as essentially leading to corruption and bad government.[2] To win, for a country like Scotland, the advantage of economic growth while avoiding the disadvantages, the seat of government must remain in a city small enough to contain a face-to-face community where people could be under one another's eye most of the time. As the example of Sparta showed, an independent Scotland would not only, by virtue of its small-nation status, be capable of a degree of public spiritedness unattainable in larger units, but when severed from England would be in a far better position to carry through the drastic state-interventions required by its neglected and backward economy. A Federal Union would thus ensure for the Scots the best of both worlds – free trade with England and her colonies to promote an economic growth which, given the scale of their country, their parliament could effectively control. As Fletcher knew, arguments of this kind, which revived the Platonic-Aristotelian principle of regarding small-scale countries as the natural homes of freedom and virtue, were likely to have a rough time in a post-revolution Scotland. Increasingly caught up in a crisis of metaphysical and moral scepticism, the Scots tended to regard the boasted objectivity of Greek ethics as filthy rags, and a cover-up for spiritual pride.[3]

Fletcher invoked the 'small is beautiful' principle of Platonic politics, and attacked the Presbyterian re-forms of the Universities.[4] The twin pillars of these reforms (the open-door policy on the one hand, and the introduction of modern philosophy on the other) far from providing a remedy for the lost standards of Scottish learning, were, Fletcher asserted, an exten-sion of the very tendencies which had brought about its ruin. The only result of the bursary schemes had been to fill the Universities with ill-prepared and opin-ionated youths better employed on farms or in workshops. To promote the revival of learning which Scotland required, the fees must be raised, the courses lengthened from four to six years, the numbers taught by one regent reduced to thirty, and – given a new type of student with money to buy books and leisure to read them – the emphasis of the curriculum should be switched as in Oxford and Cambridge to the solider sorts of learning, especially the classics, but also modern science which Fletcher admired. As for the disputatious and jargon-ridden subject of philosophy, its part in the course could probably be reduced from a quarter to a sixth, by cutting down on the inward-looking modern element in favour of Greek objectivity. Instead of trying, as in the 'printed courses' to achieve the impossible aims of holding the balance between the ancient and the modern,[5] the Universities should adopt a compendium devoted to a careful exposition of the history of ancient philosophy,[6] by way of providing intellectual background to the humanist study of classical literatures, which was to be the mainstay of the course. For the few who wanted to go into philosophy more deeply, professors should institute private classes which might study the principles of sane statesmanship by reading Aristotle's *Ethics* and *Politics* as well as some of Plato's dialogues. Fletcher sought to cure the spiritual malaise of his countrymen by state-intervention to discourage the subjectivist passion for the modern 'way of ideas',[7] in much the same way as he appealed to the 'violent' dirigiste policy of ancient city-states (forced labour and public works) as the remedy for the material ills (destitution and unemployment) arising from the individualism of the modern Christian world.

Scepticism

Fletcher's ideas were partly tried out in the Edinburgh University reform of 1708, when the controversial subject of moral philosophy was made extracurricular and optional, so as to make room for a double dose of Latin and Greek. This change attracted to Edinburgh more of the English nonconformists who were being excluded from Oxford and Cambridge, but schemes like Fletcher's for the downgrading of modern philosophy, nevertheless, soon faded out. The more useful studies of languages and mathematics began again to take second place to the thrilling debates about first principles, and the sceptical crisis, instead of passing into oblivion, reappeared with redoubled fury in the years 1713 and 1714. This was partly no doubt in reaction to the Union Parliament's check to Scotland's ecclesiastical freedom, but partly also, it is clear, because the more liberal and Lockeian section of the English dissenters who were flocking to Edinburgh and Glasgow were now asking awkward questions about the execution in 1697 of an Edinburgh student, Aikenhead, for blasphemy.[8] Faced with the reopening of the Aikenhead question, sixteen years after the young man's execution, the presbyterians closed their ranks. Their united front must have flabbergasted the nonconformist liberals from England, since the common cause which brought together proto-moderates

8

like Carstares and Principal Hadow of St Andrews into unity with proto-evangelicals like Hog of Carnock was the publication of a work by the late sainted Professor Halyburton of St Andrews against infidelity in general and Aikenhead in particular, a move calculated to plunge the whole country back once again into a morass of epistemological scepticism from which no easy egress seemed possible.[9] It seems clear enough that from the standpoint of the leaders of the Church of Scotland of the day, the blasphemy for which this remarkable youth suffered death consisted simply in the fact that he had demanded evidence for the dogma that the moral blindness of natural man can sometimes be overcome by a grace-inspired reading of the Bible.

The ambiguous entanglement of Halyburton's position with Aikenhead's can be seen even more plainly in the fragment of Halyburton's spiritual autobiography.[10] It appears that Halyburton too, in his youth, experienced a succession of similar sceptical crises, the last one (1696) contemporary with that of Aikenhead who could perhaps have been known to him personally. Halyburton, it seems, escaped from the grip of scepticism, only when it suddenly occurred to him to distrust the self-criticism of reason and to let his beliefs be guided by the inspiration of the Book. In this respect there was no difference between the St Andrews Professor of Divinity who died in his bed surrounded by pious disciples and friends, and the philosophical student of Edinburgh who died on the scaffold on the 7th January, 1797, surrounded by a squad of soldiers to prevent him being rescued by wellwishers in the crowd.

The conscience-torturing memory of the Aikenhead affair seems to have generated wave after wave of scepticism which, undermining the foundations of ethics as well as of metaphysics, brought home to the intellectually sophisticated public of Scotland the non-proveness, the logical inadequacy, of Andrew Fletcher's condemnation of the swallowing up by the larger country of the *petite patrie* as a betrayal of moral standards. Turning away from politics based on Platonic absolutes, dismissing as a chimera Fletcher's idea of a new-modelled Scotland which could unite material advance with virtue and simplicity, some brighter spirits of a new generation once again gave themselves up to torturing self-doubts of the kind which were to achieve their classic set-piece formulation, some twenty years later, in the last chapter of the fourth part of the first book of Hume's *Treatise of Human Nature.* In 1716-17 Alexander Moncrieff, a graduate student at Glasgow, who was to make his name as the intellectual champion of the first major secession from the church of Scotland known as the Original Secession, experienced what he was later to call the 'hellish temptation' to regard all the claims of religion as nothing but sheer imagination.[11] Like Halyburton before him, he found his way to faith only by a limitation of the claims of reason, and so far as philosophy was concerned he seems to have remained a sceptic, formulating a view of miracles not very different from that put forward by David Hume. Both were in agreement that the occurrence of a miracle like the changing of water into wine could not possibly be established by the kind of human testimony which is relied on by scientific history but only with the aid of superhuman testimony which might communicate itself inspirationally to readers of the holy writ.[12] Sceptic with regard to ethics as well as to metaphysics, a man like Moncrieff had no patience with Fletcherian ideas of reconciling the individualism of economic advance with a self-moderating virtue. Pronouncing on the idea of self-regulating laissez-faire as pioneered by Professor Campbell of St Andrew's in 1728, Moncrieff condemned the whole idea of economic growth as inevitably leading to a hell on earth unless it was checked and guided by a faith-inspired general assembly which, unlike modern assemblies, would not let itself be 'frightened' out of its religion by a 'scarecrow' such as Locke, with his weakly reasoned ideas about the value of toleration.[13]

The Student Societies
However, by this time the reform of university teaching carried through by Carstares in Edinburgh in 1708 was beginning to make its mark and the students were

becoming less inclined to make the sceptically based leap into religiosity of the kind Moncrieff was taking in Glasgow in the same year. It was not that they had ceased to be fascinated by scepticism and its problems, but they were taking it far more critically and intellectually. Just then (about 1718) there suddenly emerged both at Edinburgh and Glasgow student societies which, reported the pious and accurate Wodrow, were 'like to have an ill influence': they let loose their fancies in free discussion without allowing the drift of their arguments to be guided and checked by their elders.

In effect, what these young men were beginning to teach the Scots was that the double demoralisation of Aikenhead's execution and Fletcher's failure could to some extent be overcome by a patient courageous critique of the charges of illiberalism which were being brought against Scottish culture by both Locke and Sir Richard Steele.[14] On the one hand, it was conceded that Locke was perfectly right about the importance of tolerating dissent. Controversies ought to be settled by free debate, whose conclusions might be reinforced if need be by rhetorical condemnations, but they should certainly not be brought to an end by one-sided arguments which, as in the Aikenhead affair, did not allow the case for the defence to be stated and which expressed their conclusions not in public condemnations but in public executions. On the other hand, it was beginning to be clear to Rankenians, as

12

the Edinburgh Students' Society was called, that this Lockeian toleration which they admired so much was not as readily reconcilable as Locke seemed to think with the other great contribution of England which the Rankenians, in company with their professors, equally admired – the experimentalism which lay behind Newtonian theory and of which Locke had tried to formulate the philosophy. From the point of view of detached logical argument such as the Scots were beginning to cultivate, the very features which had won Locke the reputation for good sense – his cavalier dismissal of Cartesian doubt as something not worth arguing against, or his patient analysis of knotty points in the Sir Roger de Coverley passages in the *Essay on the Human Understanding*, tending to conclude in remarks about there being much to be said on both sides – had little to offer the Edinburgh students. In short the two things they most admired about Locke, his empiricist logic on the one hand and his well-meaning critique of illiberalism on the other, did not seem to be reconcilable with one another. The students of Edinburgh suddenly found a way out of this deadlock by looking over St George's Channel to the philosophy of George Berkeley,[15] which, boldly taking its stand on the slogan 'We Irishmen think otherwise' had been drawing attention to itself by putting forward the paradoxical and provocative argument that there was perhaps less difference between Locke and his illiberal opponents whether

Scottish or otherwise, than was generally supposed, and that, properly sifted and consistently developed, the experimental pragmatic principle which was Locke's greatest contribution was likely to lead men back to a God-centred philosophy not unlike that of Halyburton.

Entering into correspondence in the late twenties with Berkeley himself, who congratulated them on their understanding of his system, the Rankenians were thereby enabled to pose to themselves and to him, in a clear and discussable form, the philosophical problems presupposed by the scepticism, metaphysical and moral, in which they were so interested on account of its having caused so much trouble in their native country of Scotland, but which, on account of the crabbed and stereotyped nature of the Scottish discussions, they had never been able to examine and debate about freely until their encounter with Berkeley's fertile and free-flowing argumentation. According to Berkeley the two things which Fletcher wanted to bring together, economic growth on the one hand and virtue on the other, or in other words the problem of how a country can be rich without being corrupted, is incapable of being realised or resolved except in a society which is pervaded by God, and in which virtue is equivalent to conduct motivated by faith. Berkeley thus spelled out at length and elucidated in rational arguments positions which were hurried over by Scottish theologians of the

Halyburton type who were less interested in this world than in the next.

In their struggle with Berkeleian scepticism, the Rankenians were greatly helped by Francis Hutcheson's appointment to the Moral Philosophy chair in Glasgow in 1730. Pathfinder for the Scottish Enlightenment, who managed to persuade the evangelicals to tolerate free discussion and to leave the punishment of heresy to the justice of God, Hutcheson was already engaged in refuting Berkeley, and in thus calming the sceptical storm among the presbyterians, when Hume and Reid were junior students. His distinctive contribution was, in fact, to prepare the programme which this pair, along with his own pupil Adam Smith, were to implement, not only in philosophy, but also in its public affairs, since Hutcheson, on the temporal side, criticised the Act of Union for its failure to permit the national expression of a Scottish grievance,[16] and, on the spiritual side, criticised the patronage Act of 1712 as liable to convert the Kirk into a Presbyterian version of the Church of England.[17]

David Hume, Thomas Reid, Adam Smith
Stimulated by his Rankenian friends, Hume precociously established his position as 'by far the most illustrious philosopher and historian of the present age',[18] by showing how the Berkeleian philosophy could be properly assessed only by relating it to the

15

movement of history.[19] Fixing his attention on the question of morals and the market, he used a historical approach to challenge the theologians' view that an exchange society of competing individualists was likely to be a hell on earth compared with earlier, more intimate societies. To clear up the matter Hume pointed out that the problem at issue concerned the change from a 'belly and members' type of specialisation in a small society where cooperation was tightly organised, to a differently structured type of specialisation, characteristic of larger and more open societies, where exchanges went on between individuals in one part of the group, without directly affecting the other members of the group who were temporarily on the touch-line as spectators.[20] This historical analysis once made, it was clear to Hume that what was in question was not the disappearance of morality, but its transformation from an externalised form in which social pressure was directly applied by the others to keep a deviant in line, to an internalised ethics of conscience, in which the spectators, serving as mirrors, called the agent's attention to aspects of his behaviour hidden from himself and so made it possible for him, even in solitude, to see himself as others saw him.[21] No doubt, the moral self-criticism which thus became possible was not always effective against the abuses of the market-society, but then, according to Hume, the face-to-face society itself was also liable to moral aberrations of its own, like sloth.[22]

Continuing to interpret Berkeley's paradoxes historically, Hume suggested that the key-problem of the market-society was not ethical but intellectual. Given the fact of economic growth, the market-society could take corruption in its stride, and the real problem was how to promote 'the rise of the arts and the sciences' which kept the economic growth going.[23] The West no doubt believed itself to have the key to the mastery of nature in Galileo's union of mathematics and experiment, but not merely had no 'standard-book' then been produced containing an adequate statement of the methodology called for by Bacon and Descartes, but the production of such a 'first philosophy' was, Hume argued, impossible in principle.[24] The 'vulgar consciousness' was no doubt full of contradictions which 'the learned consciousness' pointed out, but was unable to resolve, and, in the last analysis, the latter in spite of its pretentions to lead the former, was in a way parasitic on it. The optimistic dream of Descartes or Bacon was thus without foundation.[25]

In spite of this scepticism about science, Hume was unimpressed by the evangelical claims of founding faith on the ruin of reason. Historically regarded, religion had been an unpredictable influence,[26] mainly malign,[27] though sometimes, unintentionally beneficial, as when the over-individualistic protestantism of the English, without meaning to, resulted in toleration.[28] A sane society, for Hume, would, like those in England or Holland, subordinate the Church to the

State; Scotland's 'two kingdoms' scheme was a recipe for national suicide.[29]

Hume's historical approach to philosophy established itself among the Scots as a force to be reckoned with, by the decisive influence it exercised in the crisis of 1752, when, as the result of strong parliamentary pressure to conform to the law-and-order policy which the government was seeking to make effective throughout Scotland after the Jacobite troubles,[30] the General Assembly set about more strictly enforcing the laws about patronage and toleration which had been imposed on an unwilling country forty years before. Angered at what they saw as a betrayal of presbyterian principles, the popular party sought to discredit the new Church leader Robertson, by getting at him through his friend Hume, whose philosophy of the necessity of law and order to economic growth had provided Robertson's party with its rationale;[31] and who had personally taken a hand in the parliamentary manoeuvres to pressurise the majority of the ministers into deserting the popular cause.[32] The opposition case was that, in seeking to legitimise their policy by an appeal to the *Treatise of Human Nature*,[33] the Moderates were turning their back on the part of Hume's philosophy – the epistemological scepticism – which showed him to have the root of the matter in him as far as concerned the great doctrine of man's limitedness, and were fastening instead on the part of Hume most difficult to reconcile with Chris-

18

tianity – the social determinism, according to which the proper way to end the 'sloth' which obstructs economic growth is a governmental sanctioning of the profit-motive, which 'curing one evil by another' stimulates the stagnant economy to the long-term benefit of all, by letting the irrational and self-delusive taste for luxury and status for the few become the driving force in society.[34] Outraged by Robertson's apparent sympathy with a philosophy which regards social advances as dependent on the deterministic influence of false consciousness, and not on 'a miraculous transformation of mankind' originating in man's free initiative, but achievable only with God's help, the popular party sought to discredit the moderates by appealing to Johnathan Edwards, Principal of Princeton, whose unique combinations of zeal and of intellectuality made him acceptable to both parties.[35] In the event, however, the popular attack unexpectedly backfired since a book then published by Edwards, *The Freedom of the Will*, expounded a determinism like Hume's as the only philosophy compatible with Calvinism, thus firmly ruling out the semi-Pelagianism of Samuel Clarke.[36] Instead of toppling Robertson this oblique attack on him *via* Hume legitimised the Moderates' victory. Apparently, John Calvin himself authorised the Humean view that social progress depends on the ability of the Invisible Hand to make a bad situation better by introducing into it new evils.[37]

19

From their new-found position as Calvin's genuine heirs, the Moderates were able to put the authority of the Church behind the law-and-order policy of which Hume was the spokesman. To suppress Jacobitism, they helped in forwarding the conversion of the Highlands and Islands by expounding Calvin through the medium of Gaelic.[38] So too when the Lowlands were becoming restive, the Church was able with good conscience to use Calvinism to discredit critics of the government as being Arminians (like Thomas Reid) or Socinians (like Robert Burns) who in their misplaced enthusiasm for the perfectibility of man had lost sight of the fact of original sin.

Hume and his philosophy were even more influential in temporal matters than in the spiritual. Under his guidance, the Select Society planned the new-modelling of the country's institutions to match the commercial civilisation promoted by the Union.[39] Inspired by Hume's philosophy of law to modify the Scots Law principle of a subordination of private property to public right, the temporal debate in the fifties and sixties wrestled with the problem of introducing a free market in land on the English model.

As if to redeem the intellectual honour of the nation, two rival 'answers' to Hume soon appeared, by Thomas Reid and by Adam Smith, which while building on Hume's results attacked his ambiguities. Both men began with a demolition of the sceptical element in Hume which had seemed to justify the antinomian leap of faith, Reid using a speculative geometrical approach, Smith a historical factual one. In a chapter which has astonished modern historians of science, Reid reconciled common sense and philosophy by arguing, fifty years before Riemann, that while the tangible bodies in daily experience were measurable by Euclidean geometry, the visible but out of reach items in the 'vault of heavens' were mappable by a non-Euclidean geometry of the spherical type.[40] So, too, in a deservedly admired essay on the history of astronomy, Adam Smith demystified the problem of scepticism by pointing out that the successive theories of Ptolemy, Copernicus, Tycho, Descartes and Newton all contained an inevitable element of guesswork and achieved, for a given epoch, their always temporary authority by reconciling the latest mathematical discoveries with the plain man's everyday experience of nature.

The most remarkable contribution of Smith, and of Reid to Scottish life was that their successful struggle against the vein of antinomian scepticism in Hume prepared the way for a restatement of Presbyterian values in terms comprehensible to an industrial age. Fastening on Hume's claims about the irreconcilability of the standpoints of the vulgar and the learned in regard to the Baconian approach to nature, Smith and Reid dissolved the alleged contradiction by extending to natural science Hume's principle that the key to the problem of ethical standards in a commercial age is to recognise the complementariness of the respective standpoints of the vulgar and the learned.[41] The way to harmonise the respective roles of sight, and of touch in the mastery of nature was to note that while the specialist engaged in manufacture or experiment had an incomparably deeper knowledge of the detail of the bodies involved than the spectators could have, the latter, in their turn, were in an incomparably better position than the former to compare the bodies in one given field with those in other specialities, and were thus able to correct the experts' blind spots, and even suggest to them fruitful hypotheses.[42] The answer to Humean paradox about the logical relations of sight and of touch, was, according to Reid and Smith, not to subordinate the spectatorial to the manipulative, the general to the special, as the pragmatists did, but to put them on the same level and to regard their relations as complementary, similar to those supposed to subsist between ministers and laity in Presbyterian democracy.[43]

It is in their views of history and society that Reid and Smith differed. Unhappy with commercial society Reid looked forward to a Third Age of Humanity[44] achieved by a communal effort of will, which would reinstate some of the lost virtues of the primitive.[45] Much less Utopian and more deterministic, Smith defined the dilemma of industrial society as being that of specialisation and mechanisation which although it enriched a country materially impoverished it intellectually.⁴⁶ Like his friend Hume, Smith saw the modern problem as intellectual not moral – not that of creating a paradise, but of maintaining the spirit of inventiveness required to keep civilisation alive; whereas Reid was a Harringtonian democrat.⁴⁷

In religion, a similar contrast was also present. Reid saw the Church as an ethical institution for organising the progress of the whole society, and Robertson seemed to him to be weakening its reforming influence by policies which stimulated secession by 'popular' evangelical groups.⁴⁸ By contrast, Adam Smith wanted Laissez-faire in religion and favoured secessionism in the hope that dissenting churches would restore to the newly urbanised worker that lost sense of belonging which he had previously enjoyed in his native village.⁴⁹ Far from being 'malign' as Hume had thought, religious belief thus had for Reid and Smith a function in modern society. Its undemonstrability, of which Hume made so much, was neither here nor there, for other beliefs accepted by Hume as natural and legitimate were also undemonstrable. 'Prove to me the existence of other minds,' Reid said to Hume 'and I will prove to you the existence of God.'⁵⁰

Contemporaries like Burns were more aware of what Reid and Smith had in common than where they differed. Their great value for Burns was, first, that they both liberated Scotland from the scepticism in regard to science which had constituted the intellectual stronghold of the evangelicals and, second, that in

23

their different ways they upheld the standpoint of the plain man against that of the pundits.[51] Indeed, it was only in the disestablishment controversies of nineteenth-century Scotland that the philosophical contrast between Reid and Smith became socially important. Reid was then duly adopted as the champion of the Established Church, but only after his philosophy had been narrowed down, by being stripped of its Arminian or liberal element, which students were warned against,[52] and also of that Utopianism which Reid was obliged to renounce publicly in 1794 at the age of 83.[53] By contrast, apart from supplying ammunition to the disestablishment party, Adam Smith's philosophy was broadened out in the Church-State controversies of the nineteenth century which introduced an element of free will in place of Jonathan Edwards' style of determinism which was increasingly felt to be too rigid even for Calvin.

The growth of religious seriousness from 1805 onwards coincided with a renewed appreciation of what Smith and Reid had stood for. In 1810, Dugald Stewart restored the prestige of eighteenth-century Scottish metaphysics by discrediting Jeffrey's (1804) pragmatic claim that real sciences are concerned not with 'star-gazing' but with the manipulation of bodies for industrial purposes.[54] Building on Stewart, between the twenties and the early forties Hamilton and Ferrier achieved restatements far more vigorous than Smith's or Reid's, of the principle that science depended on the cooperation of manipulative detailed analysis of bodies with a general bird's eye view of their place in the universe.[55] 'Sight', affirmed Ferrier in 1842, 'pays back every fraction of its debt to its brother sense', and, amid the break-up of the Presbyterian polity, the debate still continued as to the possibility of generalising the Presbyterian complementarity of insiders and of outsiders so as to enable post-Union Scotland to survive in an age of applied science and democratic reform.

The Argument with Andrew Fletcher

Accepting the country's loss of political independence, the Scottish Enlightenment was in its opening phase chiefly preoccupied with the great pair of problems opened by the Union – on the one hand how to commercialise the Lowlands without corrupting their presbyterian principles, and on the other hand how to presbyterianise the Highlands and Islands without corrupting their Gaelic values.[56] However, after the mid-century settlement, the experience of reorganising Scottish life suddenly began to reawaken the question of the nation's group-identity, posing it in the new form as to whether it was possible to carry through the complex task of resolving the tensions between the claims of the two-Kingdom system on the one hand and the uneven, rapidly changing pattern of the country's economic development on the other without introducing some modification into the incorporating Union which would give the Scots a more direct institutional control over their affairs.[57]

What brought the nationality-problem before the consciousness of Scottish philosophers in the fifties and sixties, at a time when the Union was at last being seen as an unquestioned success, was the fact that those arguments of Fletcher which might be dead as far as Britain was concerned were still very much alive in France. Scottish readers of the *Grande Encyclopédie* could not fail to note how the key sentence of the short dismissive article, 'Ecosse', simply consisted of a restatement of Fletcher's main point – Scotland was once redoubtable, but a small country incorporated in a large one becomes in the end venal. So too the great Rousseau was known to the Scots to be an admirer of Fletcher and even to have spoken of writing a life of him which would show up the Union Settlement as an outstanding example of the corruption associated with advanced civilisation.[58]

In Scotland, too, Fletcher was not forgotten. After the '15, much to the Government's irritation, a Jacobite version of his philosophy was evolved by the dismissed Regents of Aberdeen University and taught by them in the private schools they set up, to the lairds' sons who were to officer the '45.[59] From the Highland side too, certain poems of Alexander Macdonald burned at the Edinburgh Cross in 1752, as well as Ferguson's *Civil Society* (1767), kept alive a

Gaelic version of Fletcherism – expounded by James Macpherson in conversation with David Hume – according to which the quality of life in Scotland had been superior when it was peopled by clans and families intermittently at war with one another, uniting only to repel the foreign invader.[60] Inspired by Rousseau to restate Fletcher's critique of a metropolitan way of life, Reid's relative and friend Dr. John Gregory argued (1772) that the atomisation of life in advanced societies left no room for the fully developed humanity of men like Fingal and Ossian who both successfully combined the now specialised roles of statesman, soldier, poet and musician.[61] Appealing to the philosophy of his ally, James Beattie, Gregory diagnosed the forlorn scepticism of Hume's *Treatise* as the logical outcome of an atomistic and calculating civilisation's revolt against the inherited wholeness of a common sense which is as old as man and which received its classic formulation in the Greek philosophers so much admired by Fletcher.[62]

Having in pre-1745 publications badly underestimated the strength of Scottish Jacobitism, David Hume, as intellectual leader of Scotland in the fifties, turned his attention to Fletcher's philosophical defence of the small-nation idea.[63]

¶The Enlightenment's increasingly complex response to the nationalist idea starts from Hume's critique of Fletcher's philosophical politics. In the Middle Ages, Fletcher had said, small countries like

27

Scotland or Britanny, by growing their own food, doing their own fighting, developing their own culture, had been able to resist the encroachment of their larger neighbours, but, with the growth of overseas trade, of professional armies, and of a printed-book culture,[64] the latter had imposed their rule on the fringe-countries which were now exploited in the interests of overswollen capitals like Paris, London or Madrid.[65] Accepting Fletcher's general picture of post-Renaissance history, Hume proceeded to question the claim that the incorporation of the smaller countries inevitably stunted their development. Was not Fletcher's condemnation of the metropolis due to his classicist obsession with the contrast between the achievements of the Greek city-states in their time of freedom and their decadence after being subjected to the parasitic rule of Rome?[66] Surely, given the economic liberty present in the modern but absent in the ancient world, there were limits to the growth of a metropolis like London in relation to provincial capitals like York and Edinburgh.[67] The proper alternative to this economically self-defeating idea of a Britain drained of its resources, human and material, by an ever-expanding London was not Fletcher's idea of a Britain divided into four (or eight) statelets, which were expected by him to organise a common defence of their liberties against France without having any metropolis to organise it, but a Britain which had achieved a better balance between central and

28

regional government than was possible on the 1707 plan.[68] Given a Union properly organised, the mutual benefits to both partners would make it possible for Scotland to fare incomparably better than it would on its own.[69] Superficially attractive, the face-to-face character of small states tended, according to Hume, to make them liable to 'turbulence' from which larger states were preserved by the features so much disliked by Fletcher – the anonymity of relationships.[70]

Fletcher, Hume went on, was doubtless raising a sensible question when he asked whether or not a parliament of its own would afford a backward, 'gentleman's country' like Scotland a proper means of catching up with an advanced, 'commoner's country' like the sister nation.[71] Here too, however, Fletcher seemed to Hume to be led astray by his classicism. Drawing inspiration from Sparta, Fletcher had suggested that Scotland could make the great leap forward only by instituting a Helot system, based on forced labour for the destitute.[72] Properly organised, a Hellenic slavery-system, Fletcher claimed, might provide a more humane solution to the unemployment problem than the unregulated individualism introduced by Christianity.[73] Fletcher's attack on the only part of the Reformation-Christian heritage valued by Hume – the principle of religious and civil liberty – was, in any case, economic nonsense and calculated to retard production.[74] The way forward for Scotland was not a 'violent' interventionism on the ancient model but a relatively liberal economy such as that opened up by the Union,[75] in which Scottish enterprise would not lose sight of what was for Hume a basic fact of economic life and among the Scots too often forgotten: namely that, in the long run, in spite of all the handicaps of its situation the backward partner was, on account of its lower standard of living, likely to catch up with and even to surpass the advanced partner whose higher standard of living was going to price it out of the market.[76] The Scots could thus, according to Hume, solve their post-Union problem of group-identity in terms of a national goal, which would be cultural as well as economic, – material advance being for Hume inseparable from an intellectual 'fermentation', concerned with philosophic ideas for their own sake, and, indirectly, involving 'the whole people'.[77] Scotland could thus hope to become (for a time) the predominant partner in the Union culturally as well as industrially, and, in the former sphere, it was beginning to draw ahead.[78]

Writing when the economic transformation of Scotland was evidently beginning, Adam Smith sought to define more narrowly than his over-sanguine friend Hume the role opened out to the Scots by a Union which, though originally a leap in the dark, had unexpectedly brought 'infinite' benefits to them.[79] In the argument against Fletcher, Hume was quite mistaken in setting Scotland the goal of catching up with England. Given the survival of the spirit of

30

enterprise, it was, Smith argued, of the very essence of the improvements in manufactures which an advanced country is obliged to introduce in order to remain competitive, that the new machines made it possible to combine two things which Hume's argument supposed to be irreconcilable: an increase in wages and the reduction in the price of the article sold.[80] But while Hume was wrong in thinking that Scotland could catch up materially with England, he was right when he claimed against men like Fletcher that the Union was mutually beneficial and that the interests of the partners were complementary and not contradictory. In particular, Scotland could keep its end up in relation to England, provided that in its contribution to the common life of Britain it exploited certain advantages of a cultural and educational kind which had accrued to it partly from its presbyterian inheritance and partly through its special relation with France.[81] This historical differentia made it possible for the Scots not merely to check the tendency of the English – dangerous in a commercial nation – to rate the systematic below the intuitive, to rate Racine below Shakespeare, but also put Scotland in the position to supply the partner-country with the general ideas and the intellectual culture without which it could not maintain its economic growth but which it did not seem interested or even able to produce for itself.[82] Doubtless, this specialisation in encyclopaedia and textbook culture would not be very profitable to the Scots in a material way but it would give them a certain status in the Union, and status, after all, was, according to Smith, what human nature craved most of all.[83]

Reconsidering the Scottish question in the eighties in the light of the American breakaway, and the political awakening in Ireland, John Millar, Adam Smith's best pupil, concluded that while Hume and Smith were justified in upholding liberal economics, presbyterian education, and modern philosophy against Fletcher's classicism, they were exaggerating the benefits to Scotland of the Union. Not only was Hume, as Smith had allowed, too sanguine in his claims that the backward country would overtake the advanced one, but Smith himself according to Millar, had in the sequel fallen short on his usual clarity when he argued that the material predominance of England would be compensated for by the intellectual predominance of Scotland. Smith might be right, up to a point, in claiming that England's development of mechanical inventions capable of raising wages and cheapening products depended, to some extent, on a supply of scientific and general ideas from Scotland, which the Scots, for historical reasons, were able to produce intellectually but not to apply industrially in their own country.[84] Where Smith went wrong was in his insufficient appreciation of the difficulties involved in the assimilation by a culture as specialised and as unmetaphysical (save for poetry) as that of

England, of ideas and of intellectual routines imported from a culture like that of Scotland which, because of its peculiar economic history, was unusually generalist in its outlook and which, because of its religious history, was even at the popular level passionately addicted to metaphysical arguments about first principles.[85]

At the same time this assimilation of the smaller into the larger was not, Millar recognised, inevitable and, with his buoyant nature, he refused to rule out the possibility that the movement for parliamentary reform, then in the ascendancy, might remedy the evil. Perhaps – as his Edinburgh colleague Dugald Stewart hoped – the Union parliamentarians, before they proceeded to the expected reform of the electoral system, would modify the aristocratical bias of English education by introducing a popular element on the Scottish plan in much the same way as they were busy proposing to modify the aristocratical bias of Scots Law by introducing English juries.[86] The promotion of such a rapprochement between the value systems of England and Scotland on the eve of parliamentary self-renewal, would make it possible for the smaller nation to move into the future in more equal union with the larger, confident that the latter now shared its Reformation dream of an educated democracy.

The contributions of Millar's pupils to the convention held in Edinburgh in December 1792 for promoting the electoral reform of Westminster brought out the serious implication of his ideas.[87] The difficulty of Scotland's intellectual emphasis as compared with that of England surfaced spectacularly in the letter of fraternal greeting from the United Irishmen, some of whom were also ex-students of Millar. Having shown the world how to write history, Scotland, the Irishmen said, must show the world how to make history, by acting 'with the unity and energy of an embodied nation' in the struggle for parliamentary reform. At once however it was objected that post-Union Scotland wasn't in a position legally to take a political initiative in keeping with the initiatives it had taken intellectually: politically 'Scotland and England are but one people', and to talk of a Scottish initiative as the Irish did was high treason to the Union. To that, Thomas Muir (the most renowned lawyer-radical of the day) replied that according to the Union, the two nations might be politically one but were not spiritually one. Over and above the constitutional question – common to Scotland and to England – of democratising the post-Union parliament there was also another constitutional question purely Scottish and national – of re-democratising the Scottish Church by passing a better drafted act than the 1690 Act which had failed to prevent Scotland's losing its spiritual liberty.[88] To deny Scotland a political initiative within the Union would be, Muir said, echoing the Irishmen, 'to consider ourselves mown and melted down into another country'.[89] However, the opposition to him held its

34

ground and pointed out that Scotland, because of not possessing an independent parliament did not have the right of political initiative in the sense in which Ireland then had; and Muir, made aware that he was splitting the Reform convention, agreed to send the Irish letter back to have the dangerous passage 'smoothed'.[90] Even so, however, the discussions of the convention continued to be haunted by Millar's idea of the tension between England's claims as the predominant partner in the Union and Scotland's claims to distinctive spiritual privileges. The issue reappeared in a new form, against the background of an agreement that the reform of the Scottish electoral system could not be considered in abstraction from a general and systematic study of Scotland's position with the Union – using for its data the Statistical Account – of the country's population, trade, taxation, imports and exports, which was being collected and published by Sir John Sinclair. This organisational concern, in pushing forward the Reform campaign awakened the question of whether the Scots as Principal Robertson and Lord Hailes the historian had thought, should or should not let themselves be guided by the English. Did they not, on account of their maturity as a nation, have better founded ideas of liberty than the Scots, and historically speaking, had they not provided the Scots with such ideas of liberty as they then had? Here again, Muir, following Millar, took his stand on Scotland's intellectual progressiveness. Backward Scotland might be, materially, but 'the land where Buchanan wrote, and Fletcher spoke and Wallace fought' could not be said to be backward in its ideas of liberty.[91] And the Scots for that matter, had a distinctive tradition of political philosophy, older perhaps and deeper than that of the partner country and, if it had perhaps got a bit overlaid and even faded, that was – according to Millar – only one of the less beneficial effects of the Union.

This call for a type of reform which would give scope to Scotland's intellectual distinctiveness was not extinguished by the spread in Britain of disillusion at the behaviour of the French. After his romantic escape to France from Australia in 1796 where he had been transported after trial,[92] Muir called on his hosts to liberate the Scots who, outside the upper ranks, were pro-French, anti-Union and anti-draft, in order to let them deal democratically with their country's outstanding problems which, over and above patronage in the Church and the problem of the Highlands, now included the extension of the country's educational system to the working classes in such a way as to make it possible for every factory to support an academy.[93] So too in Glasgow in 1796, Muir's former teacher, Millar, still steadfastly anti-war and pro-reform (along with his new ex-student Lord Lauderdale) drew up – possibly as a counterblast to Tom Paine's more materialistic ideas – a very Scottish blue-print for a 'socialist' version of Adam Smith's ideas. In this, true to the spirit of David Hume and his secularised Calvinism, the principle which lay behind the moderate degree of planned redistribution of wealth was deemed an intellectual and not a moral one – that of keeping alive in the community the spirit of enterprise, and of preventing the stultification which too rigid class-divisions were supposed to bring.[94] Associating political reform with intellectual renaissance, Millar and his circle were, like Muir, heartened to see the Scottish movement for working-class libraries continuing to flourish in spite of the war.

By the time of Muir's death in 1799 and Millar's in 1801, the call for their kind of reform was being pushed into the background by the rival view of the long-lived Adam Ferguson, that most Machiavellian of Scottish thinkers, that the essential role of Scotland in regard to the Union (reformed or unreformed) was not intellectual but strategic. Going back to a part of Fletcher's scheme not so much insisted on by Millar, Ferguson pointed out that the primary advantage of the Union was not so much to enrich Scotland as to preserve British liberties from the encroachments of the centralised governments of France and Spain, whether monarchist or republican.[95] No doubt the Union, as Smith and Millar so often pointed out, in enriching Scotland and England, had also brought the evil of atomisation and dehumanisation, as the result of the specialisation essential to the wealth-producing process, but Ferguson regarded the evil of specialisation less as intellectual, in the sense of leading to drying up of intelligence, than as ethical in the sense of casting a dampener on the public spirit. According to Ferguson, life itself was the great school, and there was not much point in public arrangements for an education designed to interest the operative class in the march of science, which, in any case, to Ferguson, was self-generated through a remorseless succession of specialist inventors, stimulated to produce novelties by the pressure of competition. In such a world, where the great menace to civilisation lay in the boredom brought about by the flow of gadgets which never dried up, salvation lay in a community maintaining its morale by exerting itself politically and militarily. So far as Scotland was concerned, the defence and development of the Union depended on the spontaneous and organised excitement of the hustings at elections to a (hopefully) reformed Union parliament as well as in the drill halls and the battle-exploits of its volunteer militia, and not on the pro-Union arguments propounded by philosophers like David Hume and Adam Smith. For Ferguson deterministic ideas – in contradiction to the healthy voluntarism of Thomas Reid – sapped the public morale, by representing history as a spectacle to be enjoyed aesthetically and not as a predicament calling for decision, and their historical theories about the intellectual differentia of Scotland in relation to England – especially as developed by Millar – had threatened to produce a break-up of

38

Britain at the very time when its liberty was most menaced by the ambitions of post-Revolution France.

The Problem of Scottish Reform

Though an admirer of Millar's steadfast liberalism and to some extent himself Muir's acknowledged heir, Francis Jeffrey fought shy of their heavily intellectualised approach to the question of Scottish reform, keeping policy clear of first principles and taking a pragmatic line from 1802 to 1832 as editor of the *Edinburgh Review* and thereafter as the Liberal lord advocate in charge of the drafting of the Reform Bill (Scotland). Avoiding the complicated problem raised by Muir under Millar's influence as to the necessity of a bill which would do justice to Scotland's relations with England as being politically one but legally diverse,[96] Jeffrey was content to leave the fundamental thinking to leaders in London, and to acquiesce, under party pressure, in cobbling up in five weeks an adaptation of the English bill, which, to do proper justice to Scottish conditions, would, according to his colleague Cockburn, have required as many months to draft. No doubt, this accommodatingness exposed the Lord Advocate and the Solicitor General to the kind of charge brought by Muir at the 1792 Convention and repeated by Walter Scott about fifteen years later in reference to Jeffrey's own part in the introduction of juries – that a Scottish Reform which didn't respect the 1707 principle of diversity-in-unity would end in destroying everything that made Scotland Scottish. However, secure in the 'withering self-satisfaction' of the pragmatic standpoint evolved by Jeffrey in 1804 and reaffirmed in Macaulay's article on Bacon, the prospect of assimilation was accepted by Cockburn and Jeffrey with equanimity.

Apart from the fact that a reform which would reanimate Scottish differences would greatly complicate the social crisis aroused by the bill, there was also the general consideration that the project of keeping Scotland 'Scottish' – understood in Millar's sense of keeping Scotland 'metaphysical' – held little appeal for Edinburgh Reviewers like Cockburn and Jeffrey. No doubt, in the previous century, the tensions involved in harmonising with the Union the un-English character of Scottish religion, and the legal system based not on precedents but on innate principles, had produced a cultural spin-off of the greatest interest to the age. But in the industrial Britain of the nineteenth century, the distinctive line of Scotland intellectually seemed to Jeffrey and Cockburn to be less and less relevant, consisting as it did of armchair speculations about social evolution and of a philosophy of common sense which occupied itself in telling people in technical terms what they already knew well enough.

Yet, despite the new interpretation of the Union which saw Scotland's contribution in practical or moral terms as consisting of soldier or ships' engineers rather than philosophers, Adam Smith's ideas about the country's intellectual role within the Union, as developed in a semi-nationalist direction by Miller, remained obstinately alive. Indeed, the second round of the struggle for Scottish reform – the long drawn out problem after 1829 of promoting a liberalisation of the Scottish Church which would match the liberalisation of the British State – was argued and fought out, not in the pragmatic and offhand style which characterised the *Edinburgh Review*'s treatment of the Scottish side of the 1832 reform crisis but on the justifiability of a Scottish initiative within the Union for dealing with issues peculiar to Scotland. Indeed, the focus of the new Church and State debate, which began in 1833 as soon as the parliamentary issue was over, was nothing less than Millar's question – but posed anew in a magnified form – as to whether the Union parliament could harmonise the interests of a predominant partner which treated the spiritual as subordinate to the temporal side with those of an incorporated partner which treated the spiritual as independent of the temporal and as institutionally of equal importance. Moreover, what made the ten-year struggle leading to the disruption of the Church of Scotland in 1843 something like a repeat performance on a larger state of the tragic tensions of Scotland in the decade of the French Revolution was that, instead of treating the Church and State issue as a kind of footnote or appendix to the great battle over the Reform Act of 1832, the Scots behaved for all the world as if the Reform Bill episode were a sort of curtain-raiser to a drama of the spirit, of not only national but of international and perhaps even of cosmic significance – more than comparable to the French Revolution itself [97] – in which the Scottish nation was struggling to find a solution of the universal problems of the relation of theory to practice and of the few to the many by a restatement of the presbyterian idea of the two-kingdoms constitution in modern and popular terms. Two groups of experts were envisaged, equal in authority but independent of one another and, it was hoped, complementary, the one managing the temporal interests of the whole people as expressed in law and politics and the other the spiritual interests of the whole people as expressed in morals and faith. Caught up in this confusing amalgam of reformation religion and Victorian democracy the new generation of Scots still saw itself as the inheritor of the country's enlightenment, and intent on the spectacular realisation of the nation's spiritual role in the temporal affairs of the British Empire as it had been defined by Hume, Smith and Millar, in their argument with Reid and Ferguson over problems set by Aikenhead and Fletcher.[98] There was a deliberate attempt to remodel the intellectual legacy of the eighteenth-century philosophy for the tasks of the new century, – demolishing Jeffrey's sense of pragmatism, deflating Coleridge and German monism for going to the opposite extreme.

In other countries of the West, the Enlightenment had left behind it aspirations towards a materialistic millennium, presided over by the German monism or by Anglo-Saxon pluralism, but in Scotland it had fulfilled itself in the dream of making the reform of the Union parliament the occasion for rescuing from corruption a two-kingdoms constitution distinctive of the country, placing the spiritual order once again on a level with the temporal. Difficult enough to realise in the Florence of Savonarola or Machiavelli this idea of a balance between the sacred and the secular, between the spiritual and the temporal proved completely unresolvable in nineteenth-century Scotland, and instead of undergoing a spectacular renovation the ancient constitution broke down utterly in practice, without however being given up in theory. Elsewhere the Enlightenment may have gradually faded out, leaving behind an honoured though very controversial memory. In Scotland it went out not with a whimper but a bang and was by a sort of common consent almost instantly forgotten.[99]

Notes

1. *Glasgow University Munimenta*, ii, p. 530.
2. D. Daiches, *Andrew Fletcher Selected Writings* pp. 108-10, 136, 137.
3. See on Socrates, Professor Thomas Halyburton of St Andrews in his posthumous *Natural Religion Insufficient*, p. 101.
4. *Proposals for schools and colleges,* (Edinburgh 1704) attributed to Fletcher in *Edinburgh Bibliographical Society* vol. iv, 1901. Daiches,

Fletcher, confirms the attribution, pp. 65, 111, 132.

5. MSS Edinburgh, University Library DC41[1-2] where the arguments about the printed course scheme 1692-1697 aim at such a balance.

6. For a sharp contrast to Fletcher, see the modernism of the St Andrews Cartesians in their 1687 scheme, quoted in Dalzel, *History of Edinburgh University* ii, p. 220. MSS in Edinburgh U.L.

7. For the interest in subjectivity see John Law, the Edinburgh regent's discussion in 1696 or 97 of the infinite regress objection to the doctrine of Cartesian-type 'consciousness' in his reply to the Glasgow criticism of his pneumatology. Law was still teaching when Hume was a student.

8. Cobbet's *State-Trials* ed. Howell vol. 13, p. 916 ff. Also, Mungo Craig, *Satyr on Atheistical Deism* (Edinburgh 1696) and William Lorimer, *Two Discourses* (London, 1713) one of them the Aikenhead execution sermon, with a preface giving extenuating account of the author's part in the affair.

9. Thomas Halyburton, *Natural Religion Insufficient,* collected with other writings – e.g. the *Reason of Faith* (against Locke's rationalism) 1714, with a prefatory note by J. Hog, and an imprimatur from Carstares, Hadow and other leading Churchmen.

10. *Memoirs* 1st ed., 1714, 3rd ed., 1719 has a preface by Isaac Watts.

11. D. Young, *Memorial to Moncrieff* (1849), preface, pp. 19-24.

12. *Remarks on Professor Simson's first Libel* (1729), pp. 42-58.

13. Actually the phraseology comes from James Hunter, *Examination of Campbell* (1731) p. 14, to be echoed in Moncrieff's *Inquiry into Moral Actions* in which Campbell's scheme of selfish love is examined (1735). Archibald Campbell was reconciling Mandeville's economics with Presbyterianism.

14. For Locke, see Cobbett's *State-Trials* vol 13, under Aikenhead. The Steele references are in Gershom Carmichael, *Pufendorf* (1724) p. xiv.

15. G. E. Davie, 'Berkeley's Impact on Scottish Philosophers', *Philosophy* vol 40 1965.

16. *System of Moral Philosophy,* Book III, chap. vi, pp. 267-8.

17. *Letter to the Gentlemen of Scotland on Patronage* (1735)

18. *Wealth of Nations,* Cannan ii, p. 311.

19. N. Kemp Smith, *Philosophy of David Hume* chap. 24, pp. 537-539.

20. *Treatise of Human Nature* ed. Selby-Bigge. iii, pp. 212, 498-500, and F. A. Hayek, 'Hume's Legal and Political Philosophy' in *Studies in Philosophy, Politics and Economics.*

21. *Treatise* p. 365, and Adam Smith, *Theory of Moral Sentiments* part 3, Chapter I.

22. Hume, *Enquiries* ed. Selby-Bigge, pp. 248-249.

23. Hume, *Essays* (Oxford), p. 112 ff.
24. Hume, *Essays* 'Civil Liberty', p. 93.
25. Kemp Smith, *The Philosophy of David Hume,* pp. 547, 548 and *Treatise* ed. Selby-Bigge, pp. 213, 231, 263-266.
26. Hume, *History of Great Britain,* ed. D. Forbes, p. 144.
27. Hume, *Dialogues on Natural Religion,* ed. Kemp Smith, p. 13.
28. Hume, *Essays,* pp. 79, 80
29. Hume, *Essays, p.* 506 and *History,* p. 361.
30. N. Morren, *Annals of the General Assembly* (1739-51) pp. 193, 194, 196, 197.
31. Robertson, *Charles the Fifth* Book I, Index, under War private.
32. Mossner's *Hume,* p. 236, and N. Morren, *Annals,* pp. 376, 378. John Witherspoon, *Characteristics,* 5th ed., 1763, p. 19.
33. *Lectures on Moral Philosophy* (Princeton 1912) p. 5, Hume's scepticism saves him from the Panglossianism of Hutcheson, Kames and Dudgeon.
34. Hume, *Essays* – 'Refinement in the Arts', pp. 287-8.
35. Hume, 'Treatise', ed. Selby-Bigge, pp. 314, 362.
36. *The Freedom of the Will,* 1754.
37. Hugh Blair, *Observations on the 'Essays on Morality and Natural Religion',* 1756, revised by Wallace, Wishart, Hamilton, according to the copy in New College, Edinburgh, pp. 14-15, 20-1, 45.
38. *Scots Magazine,* 1766: Report on Religion in the Highlands.
39. N. Phillipson, 'Nationalism and Ideology'; see Bibliography.
40. Norman Daniels, *Thomas Reid's Inquiry; the Geometry of Visibles,* esp. Hilary Putman's preface.
41. Andrew Skinner, *A System of the Social Sciences*; Ralph Lindgren, *Social Philosophy of Adam Smith,* pp. 12-14, 72-78.
42. Hamilton, *Reid,* p.155, with Daniels; 'Adam Smith on the External Senses' in *Essays on Philosophical Subjects,* ed. Wightman, Bryce and Ross, pp. 161-163.
43. *Wealth of Nations,* ed. Cannan, ii, p. 304.
44. Hamilton, *Reid,* 713b.
45. James McCosh, *Scottish Philosophy,* pp. 467 and D. C. MacDonald's introduction to his edition of W. Ogilvie *Birthright in Land,* pp. 151-2 with Hamilton, *Reid,* p. 578a, and Meikle, *Scotland and the French Revolution,* p.75 note.
46. *Wealth of Nations,* Cannan, i, pp. 141, 142; ii, pp. 302, 306, Donald Winch, *Adam Smith's Politics.*
47. Hamilton's *Reid,* p. 73a, and esp. Reid's *Active Powers,* Essay 5, Chapter 5, Critique of Hume on Property, with Chapter 6 on Contracts.

45

48. Reid's views inferred from those of his disciple James Oswald, for whose moderatorial speech at the 1765 Assembly, see Appendix to Morren's *Annals,* 1752-66. It set in motion the schism debate of 1766.

49. *Wealth of Nations,* ed. Cannan ii, pp. 316-318, Adam Smith *Theory of Moral Sentiments,* ed. Raphael and MacFie, pp. 131-132, with Lindgren, *Social Philosophy,* pp. 132-152.

50. Hamilton, *Reid,* p. 461b.

51. Letter to James Tennant, *Robert Burns' Poems and Songs,* Oxford, no. 90.

52. George Hill, *Lectures on Divinity* (1821) iii pp. 99, 102; Book 4, Chapter 9.

53. 'Observations on the Dangers of Political Innovation', in *Glasgow Courier,* December 18th, 1794, summarised by A. Campbell Fraser, *Reid,* pp. 115, 116.

54. Jeffrey, *Edinburgh Review,* iii, p. 269; Dugald Stewart, *Philosophical Essays* (1810) Preliminary Dissertation, chapter 2, and Jeffrey's review in *Edinburgh Review* 1810-11.

55. Sir William Hamilton, *Lectures on Metaphysics,* ii, pp. 173-176, 144-150; J. F. Ferrier, *Lectures and Remains,* ii, p. 366 footnote; and Lectures 62 and 63 in the *Student Notes of the 1849-50 Course* in Edinburgh University Library.

56. Alexander M'Donald, Dedication, *Galick-English Vocabulary* S.P.C.K (Edinburgh 1741); Alastair Mac-Dhonuill, English Preface to *Poems in the 'ancient language of Scotland'*(Duneidiunn 1751) and *Scots Magazine* 1766, 'Report on Religion in the Highlands', Conclusion, p. 680 ff.

57. Jeffrey, *Edinburgh Review,* xxiv, p. 209.

58. Quoted in Meikle, *Scotland and the French Revolution,* p. xix, Janet Adam Smith, *Scotland in the Age of the Improvers,* p. 114. – Rousseau's enthusiasm for Fletcher's Scotland is a root-cause of the quarrel with Hume. Greig, *Letters of Hume,* p. 362.

59. Bruce Lenman, *Jacobite Rebellions,* p. 175.

60. Magnus Maclean, *Literature of the Highlands,* p. 42, Duncan Forbes', introduction to Ferguson's *Civil Society,* pp. xxxix, xl; E. Mossner, *Hume* (1970), p. 415.

61. *Comparative view of men and animals,* 5th ed. 1772, preface.

62. ibid.; C. de Rémusat, quoted in G. E. Davie, *Democratic Intellect,* p. 257.

63. Duncan Forbes, Hume's *Philosophical Politics,* p. 93.

64, D. Daiches, *Fletcher's Writings,* pp. 4-5.

65. ibid., pp. 108-9.

66. ibid., pp. 132-3

67. Hume, *Essays* (Oxford), p. 439, text in footnote.
68. Daiches, *Fletcher's Writings,* pp. 117-18, 124-7, 134-7.
69. Hume, *Essays,* pp. 501-2, 505-6, 512-3.
70. ibid., pp. 94-5, 513-5.
71. Daiches, *Fletcher's Writings,* p. 25.
72. ibid., pp. 51-3.
73. ibid., pp. 48-50.
74. Hume, *Essays,* pp. 79-80, 116, 280.
75. ibid., pp. 263-4.
76. E. Rotwein, *Hume's Economic Writings,* pp. 198-205.
77. Hume, *Essays,* pp. 136-7.
78. ibid., pp. 114-5, 568-9; *Enquiries,* ed. Selby-Bigge, p. 10.
79. *Correspondence* ed. Mossner & Ross, Glasgow edition, p. 68.
80. Early draft, p. 567 in Glasgow edition of the *Wealth of Nations,* ed. A. Skinner.
81. *Wealth of Nations* ed. Cannan, ii, pp. 294, 295, 306.
82. Letter to the editors *Edinburgh Review,* 1756 in *Adam Smith, Early Writings,* ed. R. Lindgren, pp. 9-12, 13-19.
83. *Wealth of Nations* ed. Cannan, ii, pp. 483-4 should be read in light of *Correspondence* ed. Mossner and Ross, Glasgow ed., pp. 383-4.
84. Craig's Life of Millar, in *Origin of Distinction of Ranks* 1806 pp xlvii, xlviii.
85. Millar, *History* Vol. iii, chap I, pp. 87-94.
86. Dugald Stewart, *Life of Smith* Sec 4, on the *Wealth of Nations.* Stewart's point is surely not that educated society doesn't need a democratic element but that democracy without education is insufficient.
87. Report of the 1792 Convention, Meikle, *Scotland and the French Revolution,* pp. 246-247, 257-259, and the Irish Letter in Cobbett's *State Trials,* Howell vol. 23 p. 154.
88. Meikle, *French Revolution,* p. 288.
89. The Irish letter actually said 'merged and melted down'.
90. Meikle, *French Revolution,* p. 260.
91. ibid., p. 250, with Robertson, *Charles V,* vol i, xi, ed., 1806 (Note xxv. Sec I 80 BB) and Millar, *History,* iii, p. 29.
92. Cobbett, *State Trials.*
93. Meikle's summary, *Scotland and the French Revolution,* pp. 174-176 is accurate but colourless, omitting the point about factory education, to which Mr Donelly, a student of Scottish working class history, drew my attention.
94. *Scots Chronicle* (Lauderdale's paper) 1796 May-September, *Letters of Crito* (against the war and for reform at home) and August-

47

November, *Letters of Sidney on the Inequality of Property* – both anonymous, but the former Millar's, the latter (which acknowledges his inspiration) probably by his nephew and biographer John Craig, who includes it as chap v, Vol. 2 of his *Elements of the Science of Politics* (1814).

95. Forbes' edition of *History of Civil Society* with Kettler and Hont; articles as in bibliographical note.
96. *Edinburgh Review* vol 3, pp. 156-7, 165-6.
97. D. O. Hill's Disruption picture is modelled on David's Oath in the Tennis Court.
98. Davie, *Democratic Intellect* pp. 305-312, A. L. Drummond and James Bulloch *The Scottish Church* 1688-1843 pp. 261-265 and Arthur Thomson in *Philosophy* for 1964, as well as his remarkable life of Ferrier.
99. *North British Review*, 19 (1853), pp. 340-1; Marinell Ash, *Strange Death of Scottish History* (1980).

Bibliography

On the spiritual-temporal tension which, as both Buckle (1861 and 1970) and James McCosh (1875) imply, gives the Enlightenment in Scotland its distinctive character, see William Ferguson's references to the two-kingdoms scheme of separate but coordinate jurisdictions between church and state in his *Scotland's Relations with England to 1707* (Edinburgh, 1977) and *Scotland 1689 to the Present* (Edinburgh, 1968).

The post-Union debate on its temporal side – how to promote commercial specialisation without promoting atomisation and corruption – is illuminatingly summarised in the pages on Fletcher, Ferguson, etc. in J.G.A. Pocock's *Machiavellian Moment* (Princeton, 1975) and in Istvan Hont's '"Rich country – poor country" problem in classical Scottish economics' in *Wealth and Virtue: political economy in the Scottish Enlightenment* ed. I. Hont and M. Ignatieff (Cambridge, 1980). For the tension over private property (Kames, Hume) and public responsibility (Stair, Reid, Monboddo), see Peter Stein in *the Juridical Review* 1957 and 1963. See also Nicholas Phillipson in *the Juridical Review* 1976 for the argument about entails and the public interest. For the argument about specialisation and dehumanisation (Ferguson and Reid v. Hume and Adam Smith) compare carefully Duncan Forbes' introduction to his edition of Ferguson's *Civil Society* (Edinburgh, 1966) and David Kettler in *Political Theory* Vol. 5 Nov. 1977.

The commerce and corruption debate on the temporal side has got more attention than the parallel problem on the spiritual side about original sin and the self-perfectibility of man. However, the importance of this spiritual side emerges clearly enough in two fascinating, if sometimes psychohistorical articles by Nicholas Phillipson in *City and Society in the 18th Century* (ed. P. Fritz and D. Williams, 1973) and in *Festschrift für Rainer Gruenter Herausgegenban von Bernhard*. (Fabian, Heidelberg 1978) about the metaphysical nature of Reid's and Ferguson's, and especially Beattie's disagreements, as voluntarists, with the determinism of Hume, Smith, Robertson etc. For a non-reductive understanding of the theological issues dividing Reid's Arminianism from the deterministic historicism common to Hume and to the Scottish Calvinists, see George Hill, *Lectures on Divinity* Book IV Chap. 9, and Ian D. L. Clark in *Records of Church History in Scotland* 1960-62 Vol. 14. The developing tensions between the spiritual side and the temporal are interestingly sketched by Ian D. L. Clark in 'From Protest to Reaction; the Moderate Regime from 1752 to 1802' in *Records of the Scottish Church History Society* Vol. 14 for 1960-62. The story of the two kingdom's balancing act under the Union can be carried further back in Nathanial Morren's invaluable compilation *Annals of the General Assembly 1739-1766*.

For a view of the central role of the educators, and particularly the philosophers, in keeping the two-kingdoms system alive by rendering its complicated, dualistic debates intelligible to the nation whose interests, temporal and spiritual, it was supposed to serve, and whose identity it was felt to define, see the present writer's *Dow Lecture* (University of Dundee 1973), 'The Social Significance of the Scottish Philosophy of Common Sense': 'Hume, Reid and the Passion for Ideas' in *Edinburgh in the Age of Reason* (ed. George Bruce 1967); and especially *The Democratic Intellect* (1961 and 1964), which in a sequel to the story told here, presents the 19th century church crisis as the breakdown of the spiritual-temporal synthesis worked out by Hume, Reid and Smith.

A less complicated view is to be found in Nicholas Phillipson's articles, particularly in his very stimulating survey in *The University in Society* (ed. L. Stone, Princeton 1973), 'Culture and Society in the Eighteenth Century Province: the Case of Scotland and the Scottish Enlightenment'. The function of the philosophers was not to take a central role in a two-kingdoms system, but simply to give the lead to the patricians in regard to the temporal problems of post-Union Scotland, in a dialogue in which neither the Church nor the people had much part. In Phillipson's lively 'Nationalism and Ideology' in *Government and Nationalism in Scotland* (ed. J. Wolfe, Edinburgh, 1969), the Enlightenment dialogue between patricians and intellectuals ends not with the Disruption but with Scott.

For an economic approach to the Enlightenment, see T. C. Smout, *History of the Scottish People from 1560-1830* (London, 1969). Intellectuals from Hume to Scott were not giving a lead to, but taking a lead from the propertied classes, in regard to the spiritual and the temporal. For an account of the facts on the temporal side which avoids story telling, see Duncan Forbes in *Cambridge Journal*, vols. 5 and 7 as well as his editions and his book *Hume's Philosophical Politics* (Cambridge, 1975).

The Social Significance
of the
Scottish Philosophy
of Common Sense

The Dow Lecture

Delivered before the University of Dundee
30th November 1972

As well as doing me great honour, your invitation to me to deliver a Dow Lecture on my favourite subject presents me with a great responsibility. The fact is that after being for a century shrouded in silence, part embarrassed, part prideful, Scotland's almost proverbial involvement with things philosophical seems once again in a fair way to becoming a theme of public concern and debate. Deep and increasing division of opinion has begun to appear in the army of scholars engaged in assessing the quality of Scotland's contribution to the civilisation of intellect. While specialist investigators in many lands and in many disciplines are busy playing up the value of David Hume, Adam Smith and the rest of the literati, pointing to the profundity of their views in relation to their own time, and their continuing relevance to ours, a different set of savants who prefer the all-in generalist approach – our social historians in fact – are not so enthusiastic about Scotland's intellectual quality, and they present the so-called Scottish Enlightenment, as being, despite certain merits, blinkered by the backwardness of the country and as being unable to see beyond the limited horizons of the early industrial revolution. On the one hand, we get from the departmentalised and detailed researchers the impression of Enlightenment Scotland as a hotbed of genius, while, on the other hand, the generalist historians of society, presenting the intellectual life of Scotland in terms of its economic background, give us a counter-picture of the philosophers of Scotland's golden age as already dedicated to the defence of that bleak, individualistic moralism of which perhaps we have had too much. Seen in this context, my theme for this afternoon – Scottish philosophy – directly poses the question of the crisis of national confidence which currently troubles the Scotland of our time.

Since my sympathies in this matter are, in the last analysis, not with the social historians, I had better indicate, at the outset, the large areas where I am in actual agreement with them. First, then, I have no objection whatsoever to their generalist and omnicompetent claim, with its distinctive blend of factuality and of philosophical evaluation. Indeed, I particularly welcome the insistence of Professor T. C. Smout, the *chef d'école* of the social historians, that in the intellectual ferment evoked by Scotland's traumatically rapid industrialisation, the fundamental debate about the possibility of social progress wasn't a purely Scottish affair but depended, in the last resort, on a succession of cross-border exchanges between Scotland's intellectual establishment on the one hand, and certain radical groupings, on the other, who looked, for philosophical guidance, to the progressive theoreticians of South Britain. Indeed, in his treatment of the standpoints of the opposing groups, I find Professor Smout is particularly illuminating in his presentation of the philosophy of the radicals, opening my eyes to much I had myself missed. So far I find myself in agreement, and indeed my chief and sole difference with him amounts simply to this: that I don't think he has been as successful in fathoming the point of view of Scottish common sense as he has with its Southern critics. Small as it is, this difference will, I think, provide me with the requisite vantage-point. Arguing therefore that the two sides are far more equally matched in social responsibility than he seems to think, I will try to bring out, in a new and clearer way, the real significance of the Scottish philosophy of common sense.

Let us turn at once, to the socio-ethical argument about science and economic growth which constitutes the Professor's chief justification for his assertion of the superior relevance of the radicals' philosophy to the social issues of their time as compared with the standpoint of the thinkers in the North. In an age whose problems called for a high degree of 'social and political iconoclasm'[1] (as Professor Smout phrases it), the Scottish philosophers lacked the vision to realise that the economic forces released by the gigantic industrial upsurge were going to burst through the *status quo* of a narrow restrictiveness in regard to the social arrangement of the country. Inheriting from the Calvinist tradition an unduly pessimistic view of the human condition, they couldn't easily reconcile themselves to the genial prospect that, as the Professor puts it, 'the self-sustained growth', inherent in the economic take-off, was on a sufficient scale of amplitude to dissipate for ever the Old Testament gloom and harshness by 'bringing mankind in reach of a material utopia, and by making it possible, for the first time in history, to finance a programme of social justice that will re-distribute resources to the poor and needy'.[2] Thus in complete contrast to the radical thinkers of England, who, rising to the height of the times, divined, in the socio-industrial advance, the promise of a new and unparallelled era of, as Professor Smout puts it, 'universal affluence' and 'perfect social justice', the Scottish philosophers couldn't break away from the restrictive class-bound ideas inherited from the sluggish and precarious economy of the pre-growth era, and their characteristic response, as philosophers, to this prospect of the undreamed of speed-up of the progress to affluence and to justice, was to rein it in, by imposing a cultural and intellectual discipline calculated to continue the out-dated culture-pattern of the Reformation era. No doubt, Professor Smout concedes, this tight-knit system of national education was a considerable advantage to Scotland's economic advance in the early days of industrialism, but its authoritarian intellectual style was, in the long run, a fatal legacy to the Scots, in that it sought to prolong the godly commonwealth idea into a secular age quite unsuitable to it, and to complicate hopelessly the movement towards this material utopia by the unreasonable insistence on the necessity of making its realisation depend on the attainment of a spiritual utopia too. In any case, the argument of Professor Smout and of his nineteenth-century radicals concludes, is not this Scottish idea of giving priority to the idea of a spiritual utopia putting the cart before the horse? Surely the proper procedure is first, by means of the physical division of labour of the machine technology, to solve the problem of material plenty, and then, by means of an extension of the specialisation principle to the intellectual realm, to invent an objective educational technology which will ensure all-round equality of the cultural level.

Professor Smout, it must be admitted, has given new life to the problem of Scotland's post-union performance, intellectual as well as economic, by re-examining it in terms of the vision of economic growth which the radicals evolved in the eighteenth century and which has once again been prominent in our own time. However, this bold refurbishing, by present-day parallels, of a faded ideological inheritance is a game at which two can play. Thus, judged by the kind of standard which Professor Smout sanctions, the Scottish case against the viability of this radical short-cut to a material utopia would seem to anticipate, on its side too, an idea which our age has begun to take as seriously as the idea of economic growth, viz. that a polity which postpones the spiritual or cultural problems of society in favour of an unrestricted material advance based on intensive specialisation produces the dangerous consequences of an

57

intellectual atomisation of society – the dreaded alienation. Suppose, the Scots argued, we postpone the spiritual problem so as to achieve the merely material utopia envisaged by Professor Smout and his radicals, in which science-based technology succeeds in maintaining an increasing pace of economic growth, while at the same time, as the radicals dream, the fruits of this growth are fairly distributed under the guidance of the social sciences, what has actually been brought into being turns out, upon close analysis, to be nothing but a society spiritually split between over-specialised boffins on the one hand, and unthinking proles on the other. For the Scottish thinkers, this technologico-scientific 'rationalisation' of life is not merely repellent from a moral point of view, because of its tolerating or even encouraging the intellectual backwardness of the masses, but at the same time is also inherently an unstable basis for the material progress it seeks to sustain, in that the stultification of the majority, due to their cultural apartheid, is likely by a species of sympathetic contagion to affect the mental balance of society as a whole, and so undermine the reliability of the science on which it depends. As for the radical dream of overcoming the cultural leeway by teaching-machines and educational technology, the remedy seems to the Scottish thinkers even worse than the disease since the effect would be to substitute a smooth performativeness for the inward Socratic self-examination about first

58

principles which in learned and unlearned alike, gives life a meaning. In so far, therefore, as the strategy of growth requires priorities, it seemed reasonable to the Scots to regard their complicated system of spiritual participation as a necessary component of economic advance, in that, as they understood the situation, a science-based society can maintain the intellectual standards necessary to material progress only by bridging the gap between the expert few and the lay majority and by thus making it possible for each party to keep the other up to scratch by mutual criticism, in much the same way as, under their religious system, the minister's theological supervision of the congregation was checked and balanced by the congregation's common-sense scrutiny of the minister. In this way, by adherence to the thesis that a sort of all-round spiritual participation by means of educational democracy is the precondition of material advance, and, as such, more important than the material participation based on a share-out, the Scots, as I see it, developed a powerful answer to the criticism brought against their characteristic system by Professor Smout in our time and by the philosophical radicals in the eighteenth and nineteenth centuries.

The sharp divergence of world-views, which makes it so difficult for the positivistic Professor to appreciate the standpoint of these metaphysically minded Scots emerges most plainly in his handling of the fundamental question which is central to the whole argument of his *History of the Scottish People,* and to which he returns again and again – the question which, in his own words, runs: 'What was the real and revolutionary change in the outlook of Scottish society which equipped it to undertake the technical and economic revolution at the end of the eighteenth century?'[3] The difficulty of the question doesn't consist in any lack of evidence – some sort of fundamental change of outlook is described, he tells us, by ever so many contemporaries – but rather in the ambiguity of the descriptions they offer with their bizarre and off-putting identification of economic advance with moral progress as, for example, in Sir John Sinclair's account of how the secret of the Scottish success lay in reconciling the material and the spiritual, in the sense of making 'agriculture, manufacture, commerce', on the one hand, and 'instruction, morality and liberty', on the other, 'all flourish together'.[4] For Professor Smout himself, the key to the riddle lies in seeing that these repellently moralistic accounts of economic growth are the result of a Mr Facing-both-ways attitude which manages, as he says, to have 'the best of both worlds'[5] – an apparently 'bad-faith' state of mind in which, in prolongation of the Reformation principles, 'life is still treated as a serious pilgrimage towards an objective', but in which, at the same time, under the stimulus of economic advance, and in contradiction to Reformation principles, 'the objective is not now

60

always a purely religious one',[6] but rather that of being successful in the purely secular 'spheres of intellectual, artistic and commercial achievement'.[7] But, as soon as we turn from Professor Smout's interpretation of 'this real and revolutionary change in the common outlook of society' to the often elaborate efforts of the Scottish philosophers to analyse and to found this Scottish reassessment of values, with a view to communicating its novelty to the world, the alleged confusion of the material and the spiritual, which their critics point to, suddenly vanishes from view, and what emerges from these pregnant pages (which our economic historians seem to neglect as a sort of secondary 'super-structure'), is a clearheaded and competently argued view of the opposite tensions as being complementary rather than contradictory. Take, above all, the Adam Smith doctrine, on which so many Scots, Dugald Stewart, John Millar, the Edinburgh Reviewers, lay so much stress – that while the material growth of a country requires an increasing specialisation in the practical field of production, the spiritual and intellectual growth of the country, if it is to keep up with the material growth instead of being overwhelmed by it, requires, by contrast, not the promotion but the restriction of specialisation in the theoretic field, by the encouragement, through education, of a general studies mentality which will counteract the atomisation by building a sort of intellectual bridge between all classes, including especially the new and increasingly important class of industrial operatives. Or again, consider the, in many ways, analogous platform of Thomas Reid's school – also explicitly hostile to over-specialisation – that the scientific and technical expertise required by modern civilisation will turn into an unintelligible and lifeless routine if it is allowed to develop in a departmentalised way, out of touch with the common sense of the lay populace, instead of being organised around the instinctive *a priori* which this common sense embodies. Originating with the philosophers of Scotland, and given a widespread currency by the poets and writers of the calibre of Robert Burns and James Hogg, these seminal ideas of the Scottish Enlightenment elucidate in a striking way, the paradoxical effort to conciliate opposites – specialisation, indeed individualism in the material production of society on the one hand, and anti-individualism, almost a sort of socialism, in its spiritual productivity on the other, which Professor Smout finds so puzzling when he encounters it in the characteristic claim of Sir John Sinclair as to how Scotland's triumph consisted in 'making agriculture, manufactures, commerce, instruction, morality and liberty all flourish together'.

In the light of this elucidation of the metaphysical standpoint of the Scots, it is I think, no longer possible to take very seriously our social historian's vehement claims that the social ideas of the radical thinkers south of the border faced up to the problem of

62

democratising industrial society with a consistency and boldness which puts the Scottish school of philosophy to shame. The way is thus open for the counter-proposition that, if we go back to the chief theoreticians on either side, the issue which really creates the division involves a complex confrontation, as to the metaphysical foundation of polity, between two groups each of which in its own way, has popular roots. The most general point of divergence is that, whereas Scottish democracy develops on the basis of a two-world view of man as a creature whose cognitive equipment depends on a sort of balance between an instinctive *a priori,* revealed by introspection and reflection to learned and unlearned alike, on the one hand, and the *a posteriori* facts revealed to the systematic observation and experimentation of the experts, on the other, the radicals worked out their programme of democracy in terms of a one-world philosophy of man which, in anticipation of some forms of modern behaviourism and pragmatism, was unsympathetic alike to introspection and to the natural, common sense *a priori* accessible via introspection and which for its part, regarded the thorough-going public application of the social sciences as the only possible basis for man's intellectual and moral perfection.

In the exchanges between Joseph Priestley for the radicals and Thomas Reid for the Scottish School about 1770, the metaphysical social opposition has already achieved a mature, clear-cut expression. Priestley, for example, stands revealed as an enthusiast for scientific specialisation. Inspired by his vision of the future Priestley lays it down that specialisation in scientific techniques has already in principle prepared the way for what Professor Smout calls a material utopia. 'Whatever was the beginning of this world, the end will be glorious and paradisiacal beyond what our imagination can now conceive.' Affluence will not only make life so much 'easier and more comfortable',[8] but will make selfish class-feeling unnecessary. The attainment of this earthly paradise, he goes on, depends on the perfecting of the art of education, considered as a specialised science of conditioning. 'Education, is as much an art as husbandry, as architecture or as ship-building. Now of all these arts, those stand on the foremost choice of being brought to perfection in which there is opportunity of making the most experiments and trials, and in which there is the greatest number and variety of persons engaged in making these'[9] so as to enable the testing of hypotheses. The best system of education is therefore, for Priestley and the radicals, a decentralised arrangement in which the state would permit and even encourage financially the piece-meal experimentation in living and education via co-operative communes. Imbued with these notions of promoting flexibility and diversity by way of the trial-and-error method of technological experimentation,

Priestley rejects utterly the Scottish theories of a fixed instinctive common sense as well as the centralising and uniform system of education through which they found expression. The theory of instincts as taught by Reid and his school is a disservice to science, since it implies that the central system of human belief is such as can't be manipulated experimentally. For his part, Priestley holds to the rival association or conditioning theory of Dr Hartley, which he thinks, will supply educational experimentation with a set of fruitful hypotheses.[10]

The Scottish philosophy is, of course, utterly opposed to the Priestley scheme. For the philosophers of the common-sense school the basis of knowledge and objective science isn't simply experimentation or observation in regard to bodies and behaviour, but the instinctive and fundamental fact of the conscious intellectual rapport between the members of a given society, which consists in their faculty of putting themselves at one another's point of view, and, as the phrase of both Adam Smith and Robert Burns has it, of their 'seeing themselves as others see them', in order to compare the practitioner's reports with those of the bystanders, and to check their respective bias. Different and indeed opposed as are the philosophies of Thomas Reid and of Adam Smith in many respects, they are nevertheless in agreement with one another in that for both the indispensable condition of experimental knowledge and of introspective consciousness involves this social-intellectual communication with 'other minds' (called by Reid 'social acts of mind', and by Smith 'sympathy'),[11] as understood in terms of the dualistic distinction between inner and outer, i.e. one's view of things and one's behaviour, to which ordinary language and common sense would appear to commit us. Much less optimistic than Priestley, much more aware of the atomisation threats, Smith and Reid both went on to stress that the direct consequence of the over-specialisation of civilisation is to endanger the standards of science itself, by putting obstacles in the way of the communication of one part of society with another such as occurred in rural and small-town culture in the undepartmentalised days, before the advent of industry. Thus, in sharp contrast to Joseph Priestley's hope of progressing on and on and on, up and up and up, by way of specialisation and of experiment, it is a basic doctrine of the Scottish school, bound up with their emphasis on the fundamental mystery of the 'other minds' relation, that the material progress of society is inimical to its intellectual progress, by creating a gap between the ordinary work-a-day consciousness and that of the experts, which wasn't present in a simpler epoch. Whereas for Priestley, the path of educational progress lay in promoting experiments in language reform, teaching-machines, new ways of external conditioning, the pedagogical programme of Scotland's thinkers was a much more centralised and intellectual affair, consisting in the production of authorised textbooks of a remarkable originality and power, aimed at the very necessary and very difficult task of properly elucidating the technical language of the sciences in terms of the distinctions of everyday speech. Thus, to balance these Priestleian pipe-dreams about educating the whole man and not just the mind, the Scots could point to the actual achievement of a marvellous series of textbooks – some of them on exhibition in your library – which, aiming at a real democratisation of the sciences, are surely among our country's most notable contributions to the world.

To understand best the intellectual foundations of this extreme divergence between radicals like Priestley and the Scottish school, we must I believe, go to their rival assessments of the philosophy of David Hume – whether, as the radicals thought, Hume was half-hearted in his identification with their experimentalist vision of the transformation of things, by reason of his fear of social change, or whether, as his countrymen felt, David Hume's intentions, far from identifying with the experimentalist vision, were wholly directed towards exposing its intellectual bankruptcy. Thus the radical tradition of Priestley, as crystallised by Bentham and the Mills, while it can approve of Hume's social ethics as the source from which Bentham learned that 'the cause of the people [is] the cause of virtue',[12] at the same time condemns Hume's epistemology as a betrayal of the cause of the people, because, as J. S. Mill put it, a scepticism like Hume's 'agreed very well with the comfortable classes, but not with uncomfortable classes, because the rich can get on without a faith, but the poor can't'.[13] By contrast, from the point of view of the Scottish school, Hume's sceptical queries, far from being anti-popular, had succeeded, for the first time in the history of philosophy, in vigorously posing the question of the social basis of science. For men like Adam Smith and Reid, what Hume had discovered was in effect that the utilitarian programme of economic growth, to which he, like everybody of his time, was attracted, was being endangered and undermined by being tied to a naïve scheme of science, according to which the path of progress consisted in the learned talking down to the vulgar, and correcting the complexity of their inherited ways of thought in the light of simplifying discovery. The radicals' criticism of Hume's philosophy as too pusillanimous to rise to the bright vision of the material utopia is thus offset by this alternative assessment of him as being, in the weighty words of Adam Smith 'by far the most illustrious philosopher and historian of the present age'[14] – who, as a result of painfully living through, between the ages of fifteen and 'one and twenty', a Rimbaud-like season in hell, had realised, with the insight of genius, that the social and material expansion of life was precipitating a scientific and intellectual crisis, of an

68

unparalleled nature, which could not be surmounted without 'a reversal of roles'[15] on the part of both the learned and of the vulgar, such as would make it necessary for empirical science somehow to come to terms with non-empirical common sense, and for experiment to play along with the constants of human nature instead of dreaming of transforming it out of all recognition.

But it isn't enough to show in this way that the Scottish philosophers of the eighteenth century were a match, and perhaps more than a match, for the early radical thinkers. We must also consider how far the successors of Reid and Smith and Dugald Stewart stood up to the deepening intellectual crisis of the early nineteenth century when the Utilitarians were winning over sectors of the middle class and when William Cobbett was beginning to rouse the workers. Is it true, as Professor Smout tells us, that William Cobbett was absolutely justified in his diatribes and rants against the Scottish 'feelosophy' for its inhuman policy of expecting the working man to put philosophy before food – Bacon with a capital B before bacon with a small b – as well as for its absurd principle of stressing, within education, the necessity of a so-called generalist approach to knowledge when it was perfectly obvious to Cobbett at least that general knowledge, in the general studies sense, was a nonsense and that the only practicable sort of knowledge was particular specialist knowledge, life-based and concrete? Or again is it true, as the *History of the Scottish People* tries to make out, that the introspectiveness of the Scottish philosophy had no message for the new age of the machine, when, as a result of Benthamite propaganda, there was an understandable 'decline of interest in abstract speculation' of the type favoured by the Scottish philosophers, accompanied by a corresponding 'expansion of the concrete and utilitarian studies that would help men to deal with the world as they found it'.[16] James Mill in particular was, from Professor Smout's point of view, hitting the nail on the head when, carrying forward William Cobbett's point, he argued in his essay on education, first, that it was preposterous of Scottish philosophy to give the spiritual problem of popular instruction a priority over the problems of poverty and of material distribution, and, second, that, in any case, the kind of education the Scots envisaged was too subjectively bookish as well as too Platonic to offer detailed, objectively checkable, and scientific information about the proper path to social happiness.

If we are to make real sense of the later philosophical movement from Dugald Stewart through Thomas Brown and through Sir William Hamilton up to J. F. Ferrier, 'the last of the metaphysicians', we must start with the *Edinburgh Review*, and in particular, its response to these attacks, by Cobbett and by the Utilitarians, on the irrelevance, to the new age, of the Scottish approach to philosophy and education. What we get from the *Edinburgh* is a patient and sympathetic reconsideration of what the radical critics had to say. In this way, the whole stimulus to the Scottish rethinking of the great problem of the relation of knowledge to economic growth can be traced to Francis Jeffrey's pointed and well-argued[17] claim that in the new conditions of the nineteenth century, mental philosophy was not so useful socially and educationally as the earlier Scottish Enlightenment had thought. By comparison with philosophy, experimental sciences like chemistry were making an indispensable and indisputable contribution to the economic advance, in the sense that their discoveries gave us new powers over matter, and prepared the way for manufacturing developments. Because these experimental sciences were capable of practical application as well as of theoretic excitement, there was no question in Jeffrey's mind but that they should be educationally made accessible to all classes, including the operative class, through agencies like the society for the propagation of useful knowledge as well as through extra-mural classes at the Universities. But, Jeffrey goes on, judged by such a utilitarian criterion, philosophy comes off badly, because, not being an experimental science, directed immediately or mediately to the controlled manipulation of matter, but merely an introspective or reflective analysis of common sense, it was like making a map of a district one was entirely familiar with as a pedestrian – in the sense that the sole function of philosophy lay in making explicit beliefs of which the ordinary man was, in his own way, already perfectly conscious. Thus the philosophy officially in vogue in Scotland – the descriptive philosophy of common sense and of ordinary language – was, for the sceptical Jeffrey, just as futile and unnecessary as the two revisionary philosophies with which it was locked in combat – the simplifying atomistic empiricism of these English radicals or the new metaphysical mysticism from Germany, each of them with its own peculiar dream of overthrowing common sense. In this way, Jeffrey's comparison between science as an experimental, real analysis, and philosophy as an introspective and merely logical analysis, points to a new version of Adam Smith's educational programme according to which popular science is all that is necessary to enable the general populace to appreciate the meaning and purpose of their science-based society. Philosophy isn't required to supplement science; unreflective unphilosophical common sense is enough.

If we are to do justice to the unity and power of the intellectual movement in Scotland down to 1850 and later, it is impossible, in my estimation, to exaggerate the importance of these writings of Francis Jeffrey (1804 and 1811) as a rallying point for Scottish philosophy, and a restarting of the great debate. His dismissal of reflective analysis – his claim that the unifying ground of the natural sciences was to be found in ordinary unphilosophical common sense – galvanised the Scottish intellectual establishment as nothing had done since the challenge of David Hume. A chain reaction of arguments at once was sparked off, which, lasting for some thirty years, brought in Dugald Stewart, Thomas Brown, Sir William Hamilton and J. F. Ferrier, all fighting for their altars and their fires, as the intellectual leaders of the Scots, against the philistine and anti-intellectual arguments of Francis Jeffrey, and, later, of his protégé, the youthful Macaulay. Forced to justify the social role of ideas in the new age of machinery, the Scottish school, with some aid from the physicist J. B. Forbes and the prophet Thomas Carlyle, produced a most promising restatement of the alienation and atomisation critique of modern society, which, in freshness and force, compares remarkably well with that of the generation of Adam Smith or Thomas Reid.

The central result of this complicated controversy emerges most clearly by fixing on the contribution of Sir William Hamilton.[18] Looking to the role of the reflective analysis of common sense, at a time of the material and external transformation of Scotland on a vast scale, Hamilton argued that the very point which Jeffrey and Macaulay regarded as philosophy's great weakness, the subjective inwardness of its researches, as compared with those of physical science, was

73

precisely what constituted its chief strength as well as its socio-educational value. Consider carefully, says Hamilton, the chief point made by the disparagers of philosophy, that, whereas in lectures on science, the distinctions involved in a chemical analysis can literally be shown to all the students simultaneously in a public experiment, the distinctions asserted in lectures on the philosophy of mind – as, e.g. the holistic structure of visual experience as contrasted with the atomistic structure of tactual experience – can't in a like manner be publicly exhibited. What Hamilton points out is that this private element in philosophy, far from being futile, actually serves to bring home two vital characteristics about verification in general which are apt to escape notice in the science laboratory – first, that the hearer in the philosophy class has to reflect on, to introspect, the personal side of his experiences to check on the lecturer's description of how sight differs from touch, as to whether it applies to his own case, and secondly that, in the course of this private checking, there arises a sort of tension or rapport in which students and teacher compare their intimate findings with one another. In this way, philosophy, if properly taught, makes explicit two essential features of the scientific process in general – critical reflection and critical debate – which obtain equally in physics as in philosophy, but are apt to be overlooked in the former sphere, by reason of its obtrusive and external involvement with experimental equipment. Just as in the study of mind, so in the study of matter, the extroverted work of observation and experiment presupposes a self-introverted analysis, which establishes its fundamental concepts by reflection on the appropriate part of common sense.

On the basis of his defence of the role of reflection in the sciences, Hamilton[19] goes on to clear up in a profound and balanced way, the question so bitterly at issue between himself and Thomas Brown on the value of the reductive atomistic analysis of the positivists as opposed to the non-reductive analysis of common sense philosophy. Fastening on to mathematics as the key to man's conquest of nature, Hamilton argues that there are two ways of carrying on the exact sciences – one of them, organised on the arithmetical principle of regarding the whole as the sum of its unit parts, expresses itself in artificial and technical departures from ordinary language, in which effectiveness in producing results is achieved at the price of rendering science totally mysterious to the ordinary man, whereas the alternative analysis, carried on upon the holistic or Gestaltist plan of descending from the whole to the details – as in a visual experience – keeps science in touch with common sense, on condition, however, of making it technically more cumbrous. The former method, as perfected by the great French algebraists, while it has made possible the great advances of science, nevertheless threatens, in industrial conditions, to separate the specialised scientists too much from the rest of society, thus paving the way for the social moronisation of which Adam Smith warned. It may well be, Hamilton concludes in a solemn reflection which was to influence his pupil Clerk Maxwell, that unless there is a vast educational effort to re-express the point of science in the holistic terms which can reach the general populace, society will, to its ruin, cease to identify with the science which is its moving principle.

On the intellectual side, the sombre admonitions of Hamilton were taken up and brilliantly deepened by James Frederick Ferrier.[20] What drove forward his researches, in the first place, was a kind of nightmare vision, darker than anything in Hamilton, of how the systematic extension of the methods of an over-externalised material science to the problem of man and of society pointed towards a kind of behaviouristic zombie-world in which all inwardness is suppressed, and in which, in place of the ethics of free self-examination in terms of the traditional distinctions of ordinary language, there is substituted an artificial simulation of morality in terms of purely external social pressures. For Ferrier, as for Hamilton, the chief problem of the age, as seen from a Scottish standpoint, is the socio-educational specialisation which more and more was driving a wedge between intellectual philosophy and moral philosophy, thus cutting off science from the ethics of inwardness and conscience. What the age required was, thus, first and foremost, a frank return to the pedagogic ideal which stresses that, just as philosophy can't be effectively done unless its introspective reassessment of common sense is combined with a modicum of historical and factual matter, so in the physical sciences, room must be found, side by side with their outward-looking experimentation, for an explicit acknowledgement of the need for some philosophical and reflective analysis of the relevant areas of ordinary language. Up to this point the gifted disciple, Ferrier suddenly leaps ahead of his master in an incisive attack on the behaviouristic objectivism which, both among the philosophers of radicalism and among the common-sense philistines of the *Edinburgh Review,* was the source of all these sniggering aspersions on the reliability of conscious introspection as being too subjective and too uncheckable for a scientific age. What we must not do, Ferrier says, is to fasten on to the materialist dogma, inherited from Helvetius, that the human intelligence is bound up with purely practical manipulative skills, and develops only because the hoof turns into a hand. On the contrary, the purely spectatorial sense of vision, far from being secondary to the more practical sense of touch, is actually on a level of equality with it, so that the basis of the experimental work of science is a perpetual comparing and cross-checking of the holistic and Gestaltist consciousness via sight which sees things against the background of the world, as against the more atomist perspective of manipulative touch in which our view of the whole involves something more like a build-up by summation of separate 'feels' Drawing on the fruits of the Scottish School's long and intense discussion of the relation of sight and touch, Ferrier sorts out with a sure hand, the incredible complexities of the empirically based self-knowledge which lies at the root of common sense, anticipating the insights of a Wittgenstein as to how sight by concealing the eye, gives me a very different consciousness of my bodily relation to the things I see, compared with what I get via tactual feelings with their presentation of the interval between the eye and the thing seen, and combining with this Wittgensteinian aperçu the complementary insights, due to Sartre and Merleau-Ponty, that the sight fully pays back its debt to its brother-sense of touch, because, in my situation as a tactual explorer and manipulator, the hand, which reveals things as hard and soft, doesn't reveal its presence as a hand, but is, in its turn, indebted to the counter-indications of vision for knowledge of the physical nature and whereabouts of the organ with the help of which the table or other external body reveals to feeling its palpable shape. In passages which thus combine the best insights of the modern phenomenologists with a balance quite beyond their scope, Ferrier thus attains the very summit of Scottish philosophy with this justification of the inwardness of reflective analysis as an essential

78

part, on the one hand, of the complicated task of distinguishing and correlating the intimations of sight in relation to those of actual feeling, and, on the other hand, of the equally subtle and fundamental work of checking the behaviouristic knowledge, unattainable except with your help, of myself and my comportment as 'existence for others', i.e. 'as others see me', in comparison with the Cartesian and purely private knowledge of myself as 'existence for self', (Ferrier uses the Sartrian phrases) – a knowledge attainable only from within and not open to you. In this way, more than thirty years after Jeffrey's original article in the *Edinburgh Review,* his sceptical critique of inwardness at last meets its match in *Blackwood's Magazine,* in a remarkable series of articles which in the profound resonance of their social concern, transcend their own times and point forward to ours.

As Ferrier continues and deepens the intellectual side of what we might call Hamiltonianism, so Hamilton's social critique of the atomisation of the machine age is spelled out, loud and clear, in the early essays of Thomas Carlyle [21] – the Carlyle, that is, not of Cheyne Row, but of Comely Bank – especially the *Edinburgh Review* essay 'Signs of the Times' (1829). We get in Carlyle the same dissatisfaction with Jeffrey's repudiation of reflective analysis – with the mechanistic creed, accepted equally by the radicals and the Edinburgh Reviewers, 'that, except the external, there are no true sciences, that, to the inward

79

world (if there be any), our only conceivable road is through the outward; that, in short, what cannot be investigated and understood mechanically cannot be investigated at all'. Locating the citadel and centre of this behaviouristic upsurge precisely where Hamilton located it, Carlyle draws attention to the way in which the scientific conquests of the last age in mathematics, had prepared the way for a mechanistic and extroverted style of exact sciences which dispensed altogether with the inward tool of philosophical reflection. Developing, like Hamilton, critiques which had their source in the Adam Smith circle with Joseph Black and the great Hutton, Carlyle makes the point that 'our favourite mathematics, the most highly prized exponent of all the other natural sciences, has become more and more mechanical. Excellence in what is called its higher departments depends less on natural genius than on acquired experience in wielding its machinery. Without disparaging the wonderful results which a Lagrange or Laplace educes by means of it, we may remark', Carlyle goes on, 'that their calculus, differential and integral, is little else than a more cunningly constructed arithmetical mill, where the factors being put in, are, as it were, ground into the true product, under cover, and without any effort on our part than steady turning of the handle. We have more mathematics but less mathesis', as compared with the Greeks, like Archimedes or Plato, who refused to divorce their mathematics from a

80

metaphysical reflection. Emphasising the need for a return to the introspective by a scornful sketch of the automaton-world which Ferrier too felt to be emerging – how 'we have grown mechanical in head and heart as well as hand', Carlyle's 'Signs of the Times' marvellously evokes the intellectual excitement of the pre-Disruption Edinburgh of the later 1820s and 1830s, when, as we learn from the reminiscence of John Nichol, the anti-atomisation inherited from Adam Smith was developing in the direction of the general semi-socialist critique found in *Sartor Resartus.*

In this way, by adducing simply the work of Hamilton, Ferrier and Carlyle, and without seeking extra evidence in the largely analogous contributions of Dugald Stewart, and Thomas Brown, it becomes possible at long last to put in a proper perspective the bleak hard judgement of John Stuart Mill that the reactionary nature of the Scottish philosophy in its nineteenth-century phase justifies the utter obliteration of the whole school. We may concede to Mill that, in the mid-century Disruption decades, there was some deflection and diversion of the intellectual drive, with Carlyle's thought, in the quiet of Cheyne Row, alone free to grapple with problems of socialism, while Hamilton and Ferrier, by their involvement in affairs at home, were forced to concentrate their intellectual energies on the struggle, over the fundamental principles of a Presbyterian polity, between the General Assembly as representing the spiritual powers of the Scottish people on the one hand, and the Court of Session as embodying its civil powers on the other. However, that exception made, it is difficult to see in Mill's position anything but an expression of the extreme radical partisanship which increased as he got older. Surely, when estimated by more balanced standards, this nineteenth-century Scottish re-statement in terms of a mechanical age, of the eighteenth century's anti-specialist critique, compares very well with the continuing clamour of the Radicals [22] who, even in their transition to a sort of socialism, still go on, in much the same old way, about science-based economic growth as the key to a material utopia, without seeming to realise, in the way the common-sense school did, the atomising dangers inherent in an over-technical society. Thus, without denying value to the activism of the radicals, it may nevertheless be urged that Ferrier was quite justified in charging them with treating science as an Aladdin's lamp which could be overexploited with impunity, and which could be counted on to solve all social problems without itself giving rise to any.

When then, in a final retrospect, the competing alternatives are viewed in their long historical perspective, it begins to emerge with greater and greater clarity that the issue raised between the Scottish philosophy of Common Sense and the experimental radicalism of England can't be regarded, in the way our social historians regard it, as a struggle between the powers of darkness and the powers of light, but rather expresses a deep-seated and perhaps ineradicable difference of point of view about the possibility of human perfection, which is not peculiar to the philosophy of the 1780–1850 period, but which pervades the whole of Western history for the last two thousand years. Indeed, I think Professor John Passmore of the University of Canberra is on the right lines, when in his valuable book on *The Perfectibility of Man* he suggests that the long educational debate between the outward-looking experimentalism of England, and inward-looking nativism of Scotland is a secularised continuation of the old dissension between the Calvinists of the North and the Independents of the South, in which John Locke serves as a mouthpiece for the radical puritanism of the Putney debaters, and in which David Hume, on the other side, speaks with the voice of Andrew Melville or even John Knox, as the two sides confront one another over the possibility of a pedagogy which makes all things new. 'For Hume [in contrast to the experimentalists of England], education has only a limited role in forming man's moral nature; it strengthens, though it does not create, the moral principles most deeply radicated in our constitution.' In short, Professor Passmore goes on, 'education, if Hume is right, is in some measure the secular equivalent of cooperative grace, which is neither essential to, nor does it *produce,* the moral tendencies of man'. It is not, as it is for Locke, 'the secular equivalent of prevenient grace, the grace without which men could not even *begin* to be moral, because unlike its Lockeian equivalent, it cannot perfect men whose innate passions already incline them, before education begins its work, to particular courses of action'. In this way, whereas Hume's instinctivist view of education, as developed by the line of thinkers from Adam Smith to Ferrier, reaffirms, in secular progressive terms, the Genevan doctrine of an absolute gulf between God and Man, Locke's doctrine of mind as a *tabula rasa*, capable of being wholly shaped by external moulding, opens the way to the radical vision of education as making it possible one day for man to storm the heavens and sit in the seats of the gods.

Notes

1. *History of the Scottish People 1560-1830*, p. 505.
2. Ibid., p. 241.
3. *History of the Scottish People 1560-1830*, p. 257.
4. Ibid., p. 257.
5. *History of the Scottish People 1560-1830*, p. 513.
6. Ibid., pp. 99-100.
7. Ibid., p. 239.
8. *First Principle of Government 1770*, p. 4.
9. Ibid., p. 84.
10. *An Examination of Dr Reid's Inquiry 1774*. Introduction.
11. See Maxime Chastaing's classic article 'Reid, la philosophie du sens commun et le problème de la connaissance d'autrui', *Revue Philosophique*, CXLIV (1954).
12. Bentham, *Fragment on Government* (Montague ed.), p. 154 n.
13. J. S. Mill's essay on Bentham.
14. *Wealth of Nations*, Book 5, Chap. I, Part 3, para.3.

15. N. Kemp Smith, *Philosophy of David Hume*, p. 8.
16. *History of Scottish People 1560-1830*, p. 477.
17. Francis Jeffrey's review of D. Stewart's *Life of Reid* (1804) and *Speculative Essays* (1811).
18. Hamilton, Lectures on Metaphysics, I, XXVI, XXVII.
19. Davie, *Democratic Intellect*, 2nd section, The Crisis in Science.
20. For Ferrier see Arthur Thompson's centenary article in *Philosophy* for 1964, and Davie, article on Ferrier in the *Encyclopedia of Philosophy*.
21. See Carlyle's *Reminiscences* as edited by Ian Campbell 1972, pp. 381-386.
22. See extracts in Brian Simon, *The Radical Tradition in Education* (1972).

The Discovery of Ferrier

This essay first appeared under the title 'The Making of the Shorter Ferrier', as the introduction to *Ferrier of St Andrews: an Academic Tragedy* by Arthur Thomson
(Scottish Academic Press, 1985).

The discovery of Ferrier – a name never mentioned by my teachers – in Torgny Segerstedt's then just-published *Theory of Knowledge in Scottish Philosophy* (Lund 1936) was what first awakened me to the dramatic as well as to the intellectual interest of Scottish philosophy. At once I found myself caught up in the problem as to why this St Andrews Professor of Moral Philosophy, a man closely connected with the mainstream of Scottish literature – nephew of Susan Ferrier and of Christopher North as well as father to Robert Louis Stevenson's greatest friend, Walter Ferrier – should be completely neglected in the philosophy classrooms of twentieth-century Scotland in favour of contemporaries or near contemporaries of his such as J. S. Mill or F. H. Bradley, who, whatever their merits, were in no wise his superiors in the quality of their philosophy and who – as I was to find out in my work as a student – were greatly inferior to him in the matter of anticipating and of offering illumination on the principal innovations of twentieth-century thought – American behaviourism and continental phenomenology. Seeking to resolve the problem, I argued in 1961 in *The Democratic Intellect* that the intellectual crisis of the 1850s, a spill-over into the universities of the Disruption controversies, of which the central feature was Ferrier's eclipse, marked the historic turning-point when the Scottish Universities, led by Edinburgh and Glasgow, turned their backs on their Enlightenment tradition as lead-

ers of British thought in order to content themselves
thereafter with a subaltern role. This view of the
failure to promote Ferrier, as the real starting-point
of Scotland's slide into cultural provincialism was the
chief novelty of my book, and perceptive readers of
it, like Mr Thomson, were quick to see that this
particular diagnosis of Scotland's intellectual fade-
out couldn't be adequately assessed until the case of
Ferrier was explored in all its complexity. It is thus a
remarkable experience for me to have in my hands
this study by Mr Thomson which, correcting the er-
rors and filling in gaps in the impressionistic sketch
presented by me all these years ago brings home to
the present age, with far fuller evidence than I did, the
necessity of doing belated justice to Ferrier, if ever the
Scottish Universities, and, with them, Scottish Education are to regain their intellectual self-respect, lost in
the recriminations and confusions responsible for the
failure to follow up Ferrier's philosophy.

Mr Thomson, as I remember, didn't always see
Ferrier in just this light. In the letter in which he made
himself known to me in 1961, he had even expressed
certain reservations. My reply was to direct his attention to the parts of Ferrier then commonly left unread
– the reprints of the early essays in *Blackwood's
Magazine*. The effect of my note was electric and
unforgettable. Almost by return of post he not only
endorsed in a general way the parts of the earlier
Ferrier I understood best – the five articles on percep-

tion – but went on to open my eyes to the fact that the part which I had hitherto found so difficult – the seven connected articles on the Philosophy of Consciousness (1839) were – as he went on to put it later – the most powerful contribution to the analysis of knowledge by any Scottish philosopher since David Hume's *Treatise of Human Nature* published just a century before. Already, at the very outset of his exploration of Ferrier, Mr Thomson was rediscovering for our time the quality of the *Blackwood's* articles to which De Quincey had drawn attention in his testimonial for the 1852 chair. Of all the endless attempts to elucidate and assess, in terms of a logic comprehensible to the west, the intellectual ferment beyond the Rhine associated with the names of Schelling and Hegel, Ferrier's very distinctive version of 'German philosophy refracted through a Scottish medium' stands out, head and shoulders, above the rest. As Mr Thomson demonstrates, Ferrier's German-inspired refutation of common sense realism provided British philosophy of the nineteenth century with the same sort of starting-point and stimulus as was given to twentieth-century British philosophy by the move made by G. E. Moore in the opposite direction in his *Refutation of Idealism* of 1903 in which he seeks to reinstate the common sense realism exploded by Ferrier. What gives Mr Thomson's book its fascinating historicity is his flair for discovering untapped sources which shed light on what Dr

William Ferguson has called the dark age of Scotland's history.

Most interesting of all perhaps, the lists of Ferrier's borrowings from the University Library not only reveal month by month, even week by week, the developments of his philosophical ideas, but sometimes seem to uncover the crises, even the secrets of his personal life. Or again, the verbatim notes for the 1849–50 lectures – intellectually speaking, Mr Thomson's most important find – give us at last some comprehension of the logic which prompted Ferrier's sudden shift from the psychological or phenomenological approaches followed in the *Blackwood*'s articles to the epistemology in his writing of the fifties (the word itself as well as the methods being, as the reference books show, Ferrier's invention). Ferrier's voluminous correspondence with the Blackwoods, in his dual capacity as author as well as publisher's reader, bring home to us as nothing else the difficulties of keeping alive the tradition of objective standards of criticism in a Scotland convulsed by the passions of church politics. The records of the Senatus and its committees exhibit the calls on Ferrier's time in the administrative chores in which he was so expert as well as giving us an exciting glimpse of the lobbying of Parliament by deputations of Scottish professors during the passage of the 1858 Act. So too, the catalogues of the booksale in Edinburgh after Ferrier's death vouchsafe glimpses of the range and depth of the intellectual interests of his maturity, while the literary effusions of his student days at Edinburgh and at Oxford surprisingly disclose the sincerity of Ferrier's commitment to an evangelical vein which now and then disconcertingly (for me) surfaces amid the logic of his later analysis of the human mind. Finally, Mr Thomson's sequence of discoveries was rounded off by the good fortune of finding *Academia Andreana,* which, containing the examination papers – put within hard covers by Ferrier shortly before his death – of his own class, and that of his colleague the Professor of Logic, goes far to confirm the tradition that in the days of Ferrier and of Spalding the intellectual standards maintained in the philosophy classes of St Andrews University were second to none in the West.

The richness of the data unearthed by Mr Thomson of course created its own problem, in the sense that his initial write-up of the story resulted in a typescript which would have run to a book of near 1,000 pages. My heart sank at the news but before I had time to express my concernedness, he had pushed from him his mound of papers, and had set about writing the *Shorter Ferrier* as he called it, which, with some revisions has in due course materialized as the present book. Measuring himself against the brief and by no means bad life of Ferrier done by Elizabeth Haldane in 1899 for the Famous Scots series, Mr Thomson has produced a work which, without being as long as hers, and without losing her readability, succeeds nevertheless in being a much better book. Better, I mean, not just in being a text for our times, researched in a thoroughly professional way, but in the sense of presenting Ferrier's life not in Miss Haldane's fashion as something fixed and finished, the function of which was simply to prepare the way for the superior progressiveness of Scotland's twentieth century, but as something – the very reverse of her preconceptions – which, refusing to sink itself into the background as a setting for a more mature epoch, continues to make a stand over against the Scotland of our time, challenging its sectionalizing and superficial movement of mind in the name of the consistency and standards of another and earlier Scotland. Furnishing his readers with a sufficient supply of new facts to enable them to take issue with his own sometimes audacious interpretations, Mr Thomson's short book succeeds in organizing the multifarious complicated problems of his country – in religion, education, economics, culture, nationality, family life – into a connected continuous argument, about the engaging, equivocal, exemplary personality of the forgotten figure who was by far the most powerful thinker of Scotland's nineteenth century.

However, it is one thing to prepare a readable book and quite another to get it out and get it widely read – a circumstance which brings us up against the real obstacle to the righting of the wrong done to Ferrier so long ago – namely the continuing refusal of his country's cultural establishment to acknowledge the authority of the logic-based philosophy, which, according to Ferrier, it was obligatory on the Scots to take as their guiding star, if their nation was not to founder amid the complications created for it by the peculiarities of its post-Union constitution.

Similar to the equivocal attitude so common in Scotland until very recently towards the international acclaim of the country's eighteenth-century thinkers, the Scottish blind-spot regarding the view of Ferrier as a follow-up to the Enlightenment contrasts intriguingly with the growing interest in his work elsewhere. In the USA, Professor Natanson is reissuing Ferrier's works as number one in a series (Garland Press, 1980) devoted to the theme of anticipations in nineteenth-century philosophers, of the phenomeno-logical movement of the twentieth century. In Australia, Professor Robert Brown, in his survey of *British Philosophy Between Hume and J. S. Mill* (1970 New York) has reprinted three of Ferrier's articles on perception, and it was in England that Mr Thomson's previous efforts to make Ferrier better known found their chief support. Turned down locally, his 1964 centenary article on Ferrier appeared in *Philosophy,* the journal of the Royal Institute of Philosophy in London, and it was an Oxford referee who commended as being worthy for publication his MS edition of the 1849–50 lectures which, but for hesitation at this end, would have seen the light of day. The sense of inferiority dies hard.

But, however it may have been formerly, there is something in the air of the age which keeps pushing Ferrier into prominence. No sooner was Mr Thomson thwarted in his plan for producing an edition of the manuscript materials whose main interest certainly was for the few than he bobs up again with a book which makes the problem of Ferrier accessible to many.

The difficulty of finding appropriate sponsorship for a book on a Scottish philosopher whom the Scots have preferred to forget was in due course overcome by the courage and generosity of St Andrews University whose tradition has kept alive a vague memory of Ferrier as one of the most interesting of its long line of distinguished thinkers from Laurence of Lindores in the fifteenth century to G. F. Stout in ours. But in promoting Mr Thomson's work, the ancient University is doing more than honouring its past, it is also honouring the achievement of much more recent teachers and alumni – Principal Sir James Donaldson, Professors Burnet, W. L. Lorimer and Douglas Young for example – in showing our century how it is possible to be Scottish without being provincial. It is with such sons of St Andrews that Mr Thomson belongs, and the particular virtue of his book, as I read it, consists in the effective reconciliation of what some have pronounced irreconcilable – the outspokenness of Scottish Democracy with the witty exclusive spirit of irresistible superiority characterising the Cambridge of his friends G. E. Moore and C. D. Broad – not to forget Wittgenstein. Published with the assistance of the ancient University, it is to be hoped that works such as this one by Mr Thomson will play a part in breaking the dismal tradition of pedestrianization of standards – so entertainingly analysed in Mr Thomson's pages on Ferrier and the Free Church lobby – which, with partisan promotions to Edinburgh professorships of philosophy by the Town Council, first became an established fact of Scottish life. The banal lack of vision in the passing over of the brilliant Ferrier for the 'circumlocutionist' Patrick MacDougal in 1852, and, four years later, for Alexander Campbell Fraser, *alias* 'Ramble-along-again' was in due course carried over into the twentieth century, chiefly through the complicity of Fraser's pupil and successor, the respected but rather superficial Andrew Seth Pringle-Pattison, in whose eyes the remarkable longevity of his old teacher somehow served to set the seal of divine ratification on what had at one time seemed an undeserved elevation. On the way out by now, this hang-over from the cultural blight is however still capable of resurfacing from the depths of the Scottish psyche. Witness the public patronage accorded last year to a book on education in Victorian Scotland which in order to present the chief engineer of the canvasses against Ferrier – Duncan Maclaren MP, Lord Provost of Edinburgh – as the model of a socially responsible democrat, stays completely silent about the sectarian origins of his educational influence, so memorably presented in Mr Thomson's human comedy of Scottish Society in the Victorian age.

With Mr Thomson's break-through and the wider support for Ferrier's effort to rethink Scottish values, the situation is different, Scottish philosophy is once again on the move, the writing is on the wall for unimaginative provincialism.

Scottish Philosophy and
Robertson Smith

In 1864, The year of Ferrier's death, it might have appeared and indeed to interested parties like Victor Cousin did appear that the future of the distinctive current of Scottish philosophy was reasonably secure. Of the eight professors of philosophy no less than seven in one way or another were identified with Reid and the common sense tradition. The eighth, Alexander Bain, was a Scottish disciple of utilitarianism, appointed to the new Regius Chair in Aberdeen in 1860 by a Liberal Government, who although very much respected, was uninfluential on account of his avowed agnosticism. The Scottish philosophy of common sense thus had a sort of monopoly of the field.

The intellectual status of this corps of philosophers was tolerably respectable, not only the said Bain but also Robert Flint, being men of a certain international reputation who haven't been entirely forgotten. But what weakened the general standing of Scottish philosophy in the world at large was that the academic departments not only were riven by the acrimonious disputes between the rival branches of the dismembered church, but what was worse were compromised by what we could call bad faith in reference to some of the great names of the recent past of Scottish philosophy. For example, Hamilton was claimed by both parties as a kind of pillar of the Presbyterian intellect but at the same time they were in one might say tacit agreement in hushing up the fact that before his death he had gone over to the Scottish Episcopal Church as being, with all its faults, less unfaithful to the principles of a Scottish Reformation than the embattled sectarianism of the three factions which laid rival claims to the inheritance of Andrew Melville. The same kind of embarrassing inconsistency was repeated in regard to the other thinker of some genius, Ferrier, who was coming to be accepted as the enemy of the Scottish tradition in philosophy whereas what he had been seeking to do, according to the claims made by himself in his life and borne out by the recently discovered lecture courses, was to renew the Scottish tradition, not to abolish it. Indeed, the ultimate source of his unpopularity with his countrymen was his having put forward the idea, in a retrospective judgment on the Disruption forming of the Free Church of Scotland, that the proper way out of the crisis would have been for the General Assembly to use the delegate powers of sovereignty which it originally possessed in the Scottish Constitution, to rally the Scottish people behind it as in the seventeenth century and to conduct a kind of civil disobedience campaign to compel the Parliament in London to concede a democratising form of the Church parallel to what had taken place in 1832 in regard to Scottish representation in the legislature in London. In the event, instead of rising to this intoxicating dream of a renewal of the national tradition, the Scots had institutionalised the

102

infighting of church factions as a focus of national interest converting it into a kind of game and diverting their attention from the social problems of industrialisation at the very time when they most needed to be taken seriously.

This continuing crisis of Scottish intellectual life was decisively interrupted by the sudden intervention of a group of which there is no parallel in England – the *Scoti extra Scotiam agentes* – to use Hamilton's phrase. What was meant was the Scots or half-Scots who had made their name abroad (at this time mainly in England) without however completely losing their identification with the land of their fathers. In this continuing crisis of the fifties and the sixties, the Scots outside of Scotland who took a hand in the matter were, most notably, John Stuart Mill and Thomas Carlyle who, in spite of losing their earlier mutual admiration and beginning to feel increasingly unsympathetic towards one another, were united in feeling powerful disgust at the way in which the learned class in Scotland headed by the philosophers (even Ferrier lost his head) seemed to have forgotten about the social problem as the result of their involving themselves in the religious-metaphysical power-struggles.

In J. S. Mill's case, the attack on the irresponsibility of his father's native land took the form of his elaborate and powerful *Examination of Hamilton* (1865) which pitilessly exposed the contradictions in the complicated Hamiltonian system with a view to destroying the very great respect in which it was held. Though Mill was here concerned with philosophy, in the narrow technical sense, there is no doubt that the same social motive was at work as informed his famous essays on Coleridge and Bentham. The object of these we know from F. D. Maurice to be that of exposing Scottish philosophy – Dugald Stewart's in particular – as muddle headed and over-academic, middle of the road in the worst sense, by comparison to the two extremist philosophies Germano-Coleridgian and Benthamite respectively; which, though rather unsystematic, were nevertheless concerned with the real issues of the day and not with mere scholastic debate – confused at that. Mill, for that matter, was quite explicit that the eternal verities, the unchangeable principles supposed to be embodied in the appeal to common sense by Hamilton and the other Scottish philosophers, functioned in public life as obstacles to social change of a desirable kind, and as a digging-in point of reaction

In the event Mill's book had a remarkable success, at least in England, where the reading public had become tired of having to listen to the pedantic distinctions of Scottish metaphysicians, and eagerly welcomed the resurgence of the less complicated and more down-to-earth philosophy of experience associated with Locke and Hartley which Mill was recommending. In his autobiography, published in

1872 seven years later, Mill was able to boast in a self-satisfied way that the Hamiltonian philosophy had been toppled from its throne and the reign of the Scots ended. Proud enough in his way of his Scottish intellectual inheritance Mill held that Reid and his school, as well as Reid's admirer Adam Ferguson, were inferior representatives of Scottish philosophy compared with John Millar, because the latter was in favour of redistribution and understood the social question. In Mill's eyes the real heir of the Scottish school was not Reid and company, but his father, James Mill, from whom he himself had learned his radicalism.

The runaway success of Mill's attack on the reputation of the defunct chief, Hamilton, over whose philosophical inheritance the state church and the breakaway church in Scotland were still loudly quarrelling, seems to have been well received by the younger generation in Scotland, and Mill was duly appointed Lord Rector of St Andrews in the same year, 1865. The elder generation, however, weren't so enthusiastic, and while prepared in many cases to concede to Mill that the hundred-years long reign of the Scottish philosophy of common sense was over and done with, they didn't want its place to be taken in Scotland itself by the Godless-utilitarian philosophy professed by Mill. In this crisis an active group of Scots sought a way out by taking the advice of the prophet they had shunned so long, Thomas Carlyle, that the kind of philosophy which would meet their needs – a philosophy which would combine sensitiveness to the social issue with respect for the primacy of spiritual values – was to be found in the intellectual legacy of classical German philosophy. The pioneer of the German ideas in Scotland, and indeed in Britain, was Hutcheson Stirling, a Scottish disciple of Carlyle, who had published an attack on Hamilton from the Hegelian point of view in the same year, 1865, as Mill had assailed Hamilton from the Utilitarian point of view. The next year, 1866, was the decisive one, not only because Carlyle himself was elected Lord Rector of Edinburgh University, but also because Edward Caird was appointed to the Moral Philosophy Chair in Glasgow, bringing back to his alma mater the Anglo-Hegelianism he had learned from his tutor T. H. Green at Balliol. Unlike Carlyle and Hutcheson Stirling, who were more interested in spiritual uplift than in radical politics, and who, in spite of their admiration for German thought, didn't think so badly of Reid and Stewart, Edward Caird was not only a man with leanings towards state-socialism who subsequently spent a good deal of energy organising women's trade unions on Clydeside, but in addition, had brought back from Oxford a commitment to the liberal-imperialism which in Green's case went hand-in-hand with a sort of socialism. 'Just as the history of human progress,' Caird agreed with Green, 'is the history of a few great nations to whom the other lesser nations, stagnant and backward, are subsidiary or irrelevant, so the history of philosophy is a history of a few great names among which there is only one Scottish name – that of David Hume'. According to Caird, the standard topics of Scottish philosophy which were regularly lectured on from the rostrum, Reid's theory of perception, Stewart's theory of conception, Brown's theory of causality, Adam Smith's theory of conscience, could and must be bypassed by a philosopher with a proselytising cast of mind whose mission was to persuade the Scots to forget their Presbyterian in-fighting and to unite behind the business of social betterment guided by a cautiously paternalistic state. Thus, speaking in the name of a somewhat simplified Hegelianism and passing over in contemptuous silence the name of Reid, Edward Caird proceeded to convert the youth of the west of Scotland to a philosophy which as some caustic people in Edinburgh were aware, had in some ways more in common with the real Reid[1] than it had with Hegel. In the event, Caird's moderate leftist version of Germanism was soon transcended by a new generation of Oxford Scots and William Wallace, one of Ferrier's last pupils who, like Caird, went to sit at Green's feet at Oxford and succeeded to his Chair in the eighties, becoming chief translator of Hegel into English, made no secret of his commitment to a kind of genteel and academic version of Marxism adapted

107

to the liberal-imperial ethics of Green. Friendly to Wallace in a personal way but suspicious of his Marxising Hegelianism, Caird, in hiving off from his department its traditional responsibility for political economy, made sure that the incumbent of the new Chair was a pupil of his own, William Smart, on whom Ruskin's critique of economics had made a permanent mark – as witness his *Second Thoughts of an Economist* (1916) – but who kept the Wallace influence at bay by devoting his life, on Caird's advice, to the translation and study of the Austrians, a school then internationally famous for its criticisms of Marx. In all this, Caird knew very well what he was doing since by the end of the century Marxism was as familiar as left Hegelianism in the west of Scotland[2] a fact borne out by *Philosophy and Political Economy* (1893) by James Bonar – scion of the hymn-writing family – as well as by the little book on Marxism by A. D. Lindsay, theoretician in chief for the Labour Party, not forgetting the meteoric career of John Maclean, appointed Soviet Consul in Glasgow after 1917, all of them pupils of Smart and products of the Glasgow Hegelian school.

However, the Hegelianism and Marxism of Caird's Glasgow was a minority interest which didn't seriously affect Scotland as a whole, or even the western parts until World War I. In the sixties, seventies and eighties, the intellectual life of the populace was taken up with the excitement of sectarian rivalries and it would be a mistake to suppose that the learned class stood aside altogether from these, caught up in the enthusiasm of a left-wing Hegelianism which in Caird's and even more in Jones's exposition promised all things to all men. On the contrary, Caird's 'pure' Hegelianism was checked and modified by the much more readable and much more widely read efforts of Edinburgh philosophers[3] to synthesise the German philosophy with the old Scottish philosophy of common sense. And in the country in general (and more especially in the Edinburgh area) the standards and spirit of the Scottish Enlightenment remained sufficiently alive for there to be a widespread recognition in the church as well as in the universities that the kind of Hegelianism produced in such quantities by Caird and his group of disciples was heavy, imitative and indeed bibliolatrous, the work of minds which made no secret of their belief that Hegel had more or less said the last word about everything, and that the real task of the philosopher now that the revelation to mankind had been vouchsafed via Germany wasn't to produce new ideas but to apply a ready-made social gospel; not in fact to interpret the world but to change it as Caird himself tried to do in his patient efforts to unionise female labour. In the face of this facile flood of laborious commentaries on German philosophy, memories of Scotland's past intellectual achievements reawakened. There ensued a new dawn of socially slanted historically conscious analysis very much in the old style, and the most notable feature of Scotland's cultural life in the 1875-1895 period is not the headway made by this Hegelian hangover from the German culture of fifty or sixty years earlier, or by the spreading to Scotland of a philosophical radicalism which had outlived its usefulness in England – but a remarkable rallying of the Scottish intellectual spirit which in the process of redefining eighteenth-century values so as to apply them to the nineteenth actually produced some master works not less impressive in their quality than Ferguson's *History of Civil Society* while at the same time being, I have no hesitation in saying, much more original and much bolder. In short, to assess aright the contribution of Scottish philosophical culture (in the broad sense) in the late nineteenth century, you must look out for the intellectual equivalents of an architect of international stature like Charles Rennie Mackintosh. Men of his intellectual calibre exist alright and what will perhaps be the more surprising to some, their place of origination is to be found in the very centre of the ecclesiastical turmoils which have so often been regarded inside Scotland and out as dead and boring.

The quickest way of bringing home the scope, as well as the confidence and competence, of this renewal of the old standards in the face of the challenges from Hegelianism and Utilitarianism elsewhere opposed but here acting in collaboration, is to have a look at the reaction to the age on the part of the central institution created by the Scottish Enlightenment: the Royal Society of Edinburgh. In 1862, Principal Forbes of St Andrews (Clerk Maxwell's original teacher), in the opening address of the session drew the attention of the Fellows to the transformation which had come over the status of their institution. In his youth, some forty years before the Society had still retained many traces of the great period when it ranked as one of the first of the learned societies in Europe, but nowadays, it had become, by contrast, provincial and limited. However Forbes didn't entirely despair. The important thing, if the Society were to continue to make a real contribution, was that it should not seek to vie with or imitate the specialisation of the scientific bodies of London and the great centres whose financial and other resources were incomparably greater. On the contrary, its best hope of success was to keep the various branches of science in touch with one another and at the same time continue to rally support from the sections of the laity who might be interested. In this way, it might still stay in business and even aspire to make a distinctive contribution to the march of science. In effect, what Forbes advised was that the Society should revert to its old formula of success which had stood it in such good stead not only in its prehistorical period (before its actual official foundation) when men like David Hume and Colin Maclaurin had been its secretaries, but also in the more spacious days when Hutton, Black, Adam Smith and Dugald Stewart had been its leading lights. That is to say, it should concentrate on unexplored fields of science in which breakthroughs were less the effect of expensive equipment than of methodised common sense and at the same time always keep before them the fact that science could sometimes be held up or go astray by turning its back on and paying no attention to its own history – something which could frequently happen in larger and more prosperous centres.

The tactics recommended by Forbes were to bear fruit in the controversy over Hegel and the Calculus in the late sixties. Hutcheson Stirling, the leading exponent of Hegel in Britain, who lived in Edinburgh, had publicly suggested to the Scottish scientific community that the way to solve their hereditary continuing worries about mathematical foundations was to go over to Hegel's version of Lagrange's theory of the Calculus. The suggestion was opportunely timed since Lagrange's great achievements in analysis, long neglected in Britain, were at last beginning to be appreciated and used by British scientists with a Scottish connection, notably Clerk Maxwell, and what Stirling in effect had recommended was that it might be equally profitable for the scientists of Scotland to have a look at Lagrange's philosophy of

112

mathematics as interpreted by Hegel. At once the Royal Society of Edinburgh moved into action, and a great public controversy ensued in which the anti-Hegel case was put by William Robertson Smith, nowadays remembered for his remarkable work in social anthropology to which I shall come later, but at that time the white hope of physics in Scotland. Backed by Kelvin from Glasgow and Tait from Edinburgh, as well as by the forgotten figure of Sang who was living in retirement in Edinburgh after a lifetime spent in introducing modern science to Turkey in lectures delivered in Turkish, Robertson Smith, in articles in 1870 and again in 1873, took as his starting-point the fact that Hegel's distinctive line on the Calculus was to set aside as inferior to Lagrange the Euclidean foundations of the New-tonian system as worked out by Colin Maclaurin and later confirmed on the Continent by Immanuel Kant. In what is a typical example of the internalisation of Scotticism which David Masson had forcefully advised and which was beginning to catch on, Robertson Smith never mentions the fact that the conservative line he is taking goes back to Joseph Black's comments on the philosophy of science of Lagrange and Laplace as suffering through the defect of being an immature synthesis. The French philo-sophy of mathematics which Hegel had preferred to the kind of mathematical philosophy upheld both by Kant and the Scots was, Smith said, far too nominalistic to do justice to the Euclidean geometry. That is to say, the Hegelian philosophy of geometry involves the very dubious idea that an obviously synthetic principle like a straight line is the shortest distance between two points can be legitimately treated – for the purpose of justifying it – as if it were analytically obvious in the same manner in which identities like 1 + 1 = 2, 2 + 1 = 3 are analytically obvious. By shortening the string that joins two pegs to a flat surface you can gradually reduce the curvature of the connecting cord, but surely it is no more possible to eliminate the curvature entirely by making a line less curved than it is possible to make the regular polygon circumscribing the circle and the corresponding regular polygon inscribed in the circle coincide with the circle and with one another by gradually and systematically reducing the length of the sides of the two polygons. Reverting to a position upheld long ago by Robert Simson (the father of Scottish geometry), though without mentioning his name, Robertson Smith is thus raising the old Scottish dubiety about the Cartesian project of the arithmetisation of geometry,[4] that is of reducing continuous quantity to discreet quantity. No doubt, Robertson Smith argues, there is a real problem here for modern mathematicians and logicians, but it ought in these days to be faced by reference to the question of the applicability to experience of the mathematical logic discovered by Boole. If the Scottish Hegelians are serious philosophers what they ought to do is not to go back to Hegel and Lagrange, but to address themselves to the questions raised by Boole himself in the preface to his *Treatise on Partial Differential Equations*. In the event, however, the Scottish Hegelians did no such thing, and Caird's response to Smith's papers of '70 and '73 was to make the proclamation published in the evidence of the 1876 Scottish Universities Commission, of his belief that mathematics in spite of an ancient tradition to the opposite effect was an unprofitable field for genuine students of philosophy who, if they were to study a science at all had better apply themselves to biology. Refused by Caird, Robertson Smith's challenge to raise the question of mathematical foundation in Boolean or equivalent terms has never to my knowledge been taken up by any of the subsequent Scottish philosophers, who have kept the reputation of their subject intact by refusing to take the risk of a combat with the mathematicians.

Robertson Smith's line on Hegel and the Calculus is a good example of one of the ways in which, as J. D. Forbes indicated, the intellectual traditions of a set-up like the late nineteenth-century Royal Society of Edinburgh could help the advance of science by keeping alive scientific ideas which were unfashionable elsewhere. The important point here is that 1873, the year of Robertson Smith's last paper was also the year of the publication of the *Treatise on*

Electricity and Magnetism, by Clerk Maxwell, who, at that time resident in Galloway, had the closest link with Robertson Smith's backers, Tait and Kelvin. No doubt, elsewhere in Europe great advances were going forward in logic and in arithmetic of which the present century has been the beneficiary, but the high claims made for these disciplines in our time must not lead us to forget that the fundamental breakthrough in electricity theory was made not by the pioneers of the new logic but by the scientists surrounding Robertson Smith who still upheld the primacy of Euclid. But the role of the RSE in this intellectual rallying of Scottish common sense as applied to science, in the face of the general advance of German Hegelian ideas on the one hand and that of scientific empiricism on the other, was also fruitful about the same time through the work of the same men in the other direction indicated in Forbes's 1862 address as one which might be fruitfully followed up by a learned society in the provinces which aspired to make a real contribution to living science. This other role was the creation of infant sciences – in this particular case social anthropology which arose as an offshoot of moral philosophy in the broad Scottish sense as it was cultivated in the nineteenth century in somewhat the same way as Adam Smith's economics or Ferguson's sociology also arose as by-products of the common sense moral philosophy in the Scottish eighteenth century. Somewhat as happened in the

116

case of Hegel and the Calculus issue, what galvanised the Scottish intellectuals into action, obliging them to deploy their inherited skills of intellectual analysis in temporary forgetfulness of the continuing disarray of the national spirit was another sharp challenge to the intellectual bona fides of the Scottish Enlightenment both as it had been evolved by its founding fathers and still more as it was being carried on at the present time by its nineteenth-Century epigoni especially in the RSE. In this case the source of the philosophical revival was the challenge to the intellectual honour of Scotland which was not only implicit in Hutcheson Stirling's description of Sir William Hamilton as disingenuous because of his lack of sympathy for Hegel or in Mill's attack on the appeal to common sense principles admitted *semper ubique ad omnibus* as an obstruction to progress and treason to the modern spirit, but which had been spelled out with brutal frankness before the whole of the west in the accusations contained in the third volume of Buckle's best-selling *History of Civilisation* to the effect that the learned class in Scotland, more especially in the nineteenth century but also in the eighteenth century had been a bunch of hypocrites who, for lack of moral courage, had publicly defended the outlandish prejudices of the vulgar mass of the Scottish evangelicals in morals and religion, or at least connived with them for the sake of avoiding social embarrassment.

117

In this revival of Scottish intellectuality which answered the accusations of disingenuity and hypocrisy not by a fusillade of words, in the debating society manner, but by the intellectual deed of opening up to frank and bold examination the very area in regard to which the Scottish thinkers were accused of being hypocritically silent – that of morals and religion – Robertson Smith once again was the foremost protagonist building, however, on the work done in the sixties and early seventies, by his friend, J. F. Maclennan, at that time an advocate living in Edinburgh. The prime mover in the affair, and a man of undoubted genius, the starting-point of Maclennan was the comments on his book-length article on law in the eighth edition of the Encyclopaedia Britannica which are contained in a testimonial[5] from J. S. Mill in favour of his application for the Chair of Public Law in Edinburgh University. It was, Mill said, a commendable bit of work almost worthy of his own father, James Mill whose utilitarian point of view it applied to law, but at the same time there was a weakness in certain parts of it which Maclennan, however, could mend by looking into the patriarchal foundations of ancient law as expounded in a recent book under that name, published in 1861 – after Maclennan's article – by Sir Henry Maine, a servant of the Raj who hailed from Melrose. In the event, instead of doing what Mill hoped – producing a view of legal history which combined Mill père's view of

118

the progress of civilisation as depending on the rational reconstruction of institutions on utilitarian lines, with Sir Henry Maine's view of the origin of civilisation as depending on the authority of a father-figure modelled on Mill père, Maclennan moved in precisely the opposite direction, in a book called *Ancient Marriage*. The decisive starting-point of organised civilisation is ascribed by Maclennan not to Maine's primitive patriarchy but to a primitive matriarchy. Published in 1865 (the very year of Mill's destructive *Examination of Hamilton*) and written, one might almost think, as a sort of counterblast to Mill, Maclennan's *Ancient Marriage,* unlike his dissertation on law, makes no appeal to the utilitarian theories of the progress of civilisation as put forward by Comte and the Mills, and indeed, in striking contrast to what he did before, makes no mention of their names whatsoever. Instead, on the very last page of his book when he is making it explicit that his real theme is the speculation about the origins of the incest taboo he suddenly, in his very last sentence, invokes the name of authority of Dugald Stewart – one of the Scottish philosophers whose continuing influence Mill had been particularly concerned to destroy – and, quoting from the famous passage in Stewart's *Life of Adam Smith,* directs his readers' attention to the fact that the method of research followed in *Ancient Marriage* has been to exhibit the progress of civilisation as arising not out of changes

119

consciously introduced for utilitarian reasons, but from the operation of the principle of unintended consequences as applied in the conjectural history written by John Millar, Adam Smith and others.

As if to clear Scottish moral philosophy from the charge of a mealymouthed gentility which is afraid to face up to the ugliness of social reality, Maclennan takes as the starting-point of his speculation a state of affairs which even our modern age, untrammelled by convention as it is, tends to avert its gaze from – the grim fact of female infanticide among primitive communities which, carried out with the conscious aim of keeping down the numbers of the group to suit its economic circumstances, has the long-run unintended effect of creating a scarcity of women and thus a rise in the value of women as compared with men, and therewith a set of social arrangements involving matriarchy, polyandry and exogamy. In Maclennan's speculative reconstruction of prehistory according to the formula of the Scottish Enlightenment, this scarcity of women in a given group, combined with the domineering position which this scarcity gives them in reference to the menfolk of the group, leads these males to seek to form marital unions with the women of some other adjacent group who find it easier to maintain their scarcity condition predominance in their own group by forming polyandrous unions with a few males from the other group on condition that these latter continue to live

120

in their own group and visit them at prearranged intervals so as to get a share of their favours. In this way the women can maintain both their dignity and their independence both in regard to the menfolk of their own group and also in regard to their husbands from the other group. By a further operation of the principle of unintended consequences this state of affairs leads to the regular institution of exogamy as between a group of adjacent tribes in which the women of a given tribe intermarry not with their fellow tribesmen but with the males of these other tribes who in time come to live within the tribal group of their women. By a fresh operation of the unintended consequences principle, which in this case is connected with the transition from primitive communism to the beginning of private property, the exogamous arrangements alter their form. Instead of the husbands coming to the group habitations where their wives were brought up and live, the women now go to live in their husbands' group and the natural desire of the man that his children should inherit his wealth leads to a situation in which polyandry becomes impossible and a man has one or two wives on a regular basis living with him. Finally, by the emergence of a new set of conditions created by a further operation of the unintended consequences principle, which however happens only in special cases – where one of the intermarrying groups experiences an advance in economic growth markedly superior to that of its partners – various facts connected with its rise of population, especially the influx of women from other tribes, will make that group sufficiently heterogeneous in its population-composition to observe its own exogamy roles – its menfolk to marry only with women of external origin, direct or indirect – without going outside the borders of its economic community and without importing women from the groups which used to be its partners in the exogamy schemes. The important consequence of this situation, for Maclennan, is that a tribe, so situated may, in order to preserve for itself the economic advantages it had achieved in relation to the groups formerly intermarrying with it, cut itself off from these latter, establishing a state of affairs which Maclennan calls endogamy, and in the process constituting itself a kind of exclusive group with master-race ideas about itself. Starting with the primary idea of groups which keep their economics going by means of female infanticide, Maclennan speculatively reconstructs the course of human progress or history, from the matriarchal exogamy of the time of primitive communal production through the intermediate stage of patriarchal exogamy as necessitated by the introduction of private property, to a further stage – containing in germ the kind of civilisation we still have – which involved the break-up of the inter-group marriage arrangements when one of the constituent subgroups as the result of some

122

increasing prosperity, real or fancied, peculiar to itself, gives itself the exclusive status of a chosen people, while the other member groups continue to intermarry as before, but have the new status of 'lesser breeds'.

The speculative boldness of Maclennan's theory shocked many sections of society both in Britain and outside it. It made clear to the world that the Calvinist civilisation of Scotland, far from averting its eyes from the 'facts of life', could be ultra-realistic in regard to the role of sex in history. In consequence, he not only lost his practice as an advocate in Edinburgh, but he aroused strong opposition in certain left-wing circles, and is best remembered today on account of the long and violent attack on his views contained in the fourth edition of Engels' *The Origin of the Family*. In this controversy with the communists, the chief issue is the origin of the incest taboo. Whether as Engels holds (following the American anthropologist, the Marxist-minded Morgan) the anti-incest rules are in the last resort the result of governmental planning which systematises the results of the widespread experience that interbreeding weakens the survival power of groups, or whether as Maclennan holds it develops in a *laissez-faire* manner, as a sort of side effect of the practice of female infanticide, taking different forms with each of Adam Smith's four stages of economic development, without being influenced or systematised in light of the idea of the dangers of interbreeding which, true or false, represents the modern point of view. It is in the course of repelling the attacks of Morgan, that Maclennan in 1870 introduces the remarkable footnote in which he proclaims his solidarity with the ideas of the Scottish Enlightenment, pointing out that the only historical method adequate to explaining the facts behind the incest taboo is that followed by John Millar of Glasgow in his speculations entitled *Origin of the Distinction of Ranks* (1722) on the changing role of women in civilisation – namely, the method of speculation by reference to unintended consequences.

Thoroughly disapproving of the Millar-Maclennan theory, because of its controverting the principle of the essential equality of the sexes which – according to Marxism – must have obtained within the primitive communes, Engels seeks to convict it of a contradiction in its fundamental principle. Where Maclennan goes wrong is in using the contrast which he introduced into anthropology, between exogamy and endogamy, to refer to different kinds of society, whereas Morgan is self-evidently right in holding that exogamy and endogamy are logically complementary, that they refer to inseparable aspects present even in every single isolated society – to the fact that there is always a ban on marriages between men and women who stand in certain family relations, however these relations may vary from civilisation to civilisation. No reply came from Maclennan who had been already dead for about six years when Engels in and around 1891 made his criticisms which since then have been commonly accepted by anthropologists, for example, Lévi-Strauss in the *Savage Mind*. However, as I read Maclennan's book, it seems to tell a very different story from what the anthropologists attribute to it. What Maclennan is consciously seeking to do is to work out in relation to the history of marriage customs the distinction between what has been called in our time an open society and a closed society, the latter being a society in which in consequence of it having achieved an appropriate population-diversity combined with some material or spiritual superiority, real or fancied, by reference to other societies in its group, the government, so to speak, forbids its citizens to intermarry with foreigners.

In view of what Maclennan says, in the course of the same discussion about homogeneity and heterogeneity as being inseparable aspects of the same group which can nevertheless vary in their relationship, he may fairly be presumed to have been perfectly aware on his own account, without needing to be put right by experts in the Hegelian dialectic, of the complementarity, in a certain sense, of endogamy and exogamy. Maclennan, that is to say, would have subscribed to, or have no difficulty in fitting into his system the remark of Lévi-Strauss that 'apart from

the modicum of exogamy resulting from the prohib-
ited degrees European peasant societies practised
strict local endogamy'. It is not, however, this sense
of 'endogamous' that Maclennan has in view when
he calls his closed societies endogamous, but rather to
the exclusiveness in regard to the other societies
which results from their self-sufficiency. Maclennan
perhaps misleads Engels and company by speaking of
his chosen peoples as 'castes' in spite of the fact that
unlike 'castes' in the modern sense they formed an
independent grouping from the economic point of
view. However, the main reason for Engels' hostility
is not Maclennan's use of the word 'caste', the meaning of which, as appears from Lévi-Strauss, varied
greatly among the pioneer anthropologists of the
nineteenth century, but the fact that whereas for a
Marxist like Engels, the norm is equality in the
relations both of the nations and of the sexes, for
Maclennan on the other hand with his Adam Smith-
Calvinist background, the norm envisages a sort of
struggle between the sexes in which matriarchy
alternates with patriarchy, and in the international
field a competition within groups in which certain
groups aspire to be privileged and superior.

But even if the distinctive theory of progress inherited from Adam Smith, Millar, Ferguson and the
rest – that is, the theory of the invisible hand – might
be acquitted in the light of Maclennan's work from
the charge of implying an unrealistic and roseate view

126

of human nature in the matter of sexual ethics, the learned class in Scotland still laboured under Buckle's accusation of being hypocrites in the matter of religion: afraid to face up to the facts. What was in question here was the middle of the road, apparently fence-sitting attitude to religion which Scottish philosophy has steadily held to amid all the turmoils which convulsed post-Disruption Scotland in regard to the conflict of genesis with geology, as well as of church with state. In particular, the philosophical exponents of the moderate tradition of some sort of commonsense dualism – and such men of course were found not just in what remained of the Established Church but also in the ranks of its two rivals, the Frees, and the United Presbyterians – seemed to compare unfavourably, from an intellectual point of view both with the standpoint of the evangelicals and with what is normally taken as opposite to it, the secular standpoint of agnosticism and atheism. The evangelicals and the atheists had the advantage of starting from a clear-cut premise which they held in common that religion in the sense in which it was understood in Scotland, was incapable of rational grounding and that belief must be either founded on accepting the claims of miraculous and inexplicable interventions in human life from without or given up altogether. By contrast with this sharply defined either-or, the moderates (in the philosophical sense) were at a disadvantage in that they objected to both extremes without explaining the sense in which genuine religion could be rationally grounded in human nature. In their wrestle with David Hume, which constituted the proving ground of all the Scottish philosophers, the middle of the road men we are concerned with sought to reject Hume's position that whereas the principles of ethics and of physics had some foundation in common sense, the religious claims when considered in all their variety seemed to have no foundation in common sense, but so far the men we are concerned with had never answered Hume on the point, let alone get the length of explaining in what sense religion – and particularly the kind of religion they upheld, the Calvinist-Presbyterian form of Christianity – had a privileged position over other sects and even world religions from the common sense point of view.

In meeting the problem posed by Hume, the dualists of Scottish philosophy were committed to the task of distinguishing their position from the ethical-rationalist theory of the foundations of religion and human nature which was of Kantian inspiration but which at that time had been taken over and made their own by the Scottish Hegelians. These latter might be state-socialists like Edward Caird or semi-Marxists like Wallace, but they both were exponents of the position that organised belief of the Christian kind had the function of keeping alive, in a halfconscious, perhaps perverted, form, mankind's animating dream of the heaven on earth of an all-embracing social Utopia. The defect of this reduction of religion to ethics was of course that it left out of view the 'religious affections' which evangelicals like Jonathan Edwards drew attention to. In facing up to the problem of the common sense foundations of religion and thus of answering Hume's denial of its common sense foundations Scottish philosophy was confronted with the task of making sense of the awareness of the 'numinous', of the religious thrill or superstitious horror, as the case may be.

This challenge to the Scottish moderates to refute the charge of being hypocrites, by producing a theory of religion which would exhibit its foundations in human nature or common sense, without making nonsense of the metaphysical claims made in the creed of the churches the way that the Hegelianised religion of Caird seemed to do was taken up by Maclennan's closest friend and intellectual disciple, William Robertson Smith, who having finished with his criticism of the Hegelian idea of the foundation of the Calculus as well as with writing papers on electricity theory, had found an outlet for his polymathic genius, first in a Chair in Old Testament in the Free Church College in Aberdeen and later as general editor of the great ninth edition of the Encyclopaedia Britannica. In his book *The Religion of the Semites*, first put over to the world in a series of public lectures in Aberdeen in 1889, Robertson Smith had brought new life to the fading cause of the social philosophy of the Scottish school by employing the theory of the invisible hand with a boldness outmatching that of his friend, in order to argue in a deeply learned and remarkable persuasive way that the special, indeed privileged, claims of the family of religions to which Christianity belongs depends on their having preserved in their ritual better than the other comparable kinds of faith, what was true and genuinely valuable in the cannibalistic religious practice of primitive tribes, while, at the same time criticising and disentangling the confusion between spirit and matter under which primitive religion laboured through its failure to draw the appropriate distinctions. By a speculative reconstruction of previous history, carried on by a method similar to that which Maclennan had drawn attention to in the quotation from Dugald Stewart which concludes *Ancient Marriage,* Robertson Smith starts from the position that the life-arrangements of a primitive tribe (which he agrees with Maclennan to have been matriarchal) are conducted on a dualistic principle according to which the tribe, by turns, engages itself in the communal activities of getting its living and repelling the encroachment of rival tribes. But, this practical part of the tribal life is punctuated at regular intervals when it turns in on itself in communal contemplation in which its members not merely reflect on the past performances of their group with a view to the tribe's survival but at the same time recreate their feeling of tribal unity and their faith in the tribe's future by the taking of a ritual meal. What gives this ceremonial meal a character at once awesome and exhilarating was not just that it was the only occasion – to begin with – in which the mainly vegetarian tribe partook of flesh but more especially that the flesh they consumed and the blood they drank were those of a species of living being whose blood on other than these sacred occasions it was absolutely forbidden to shed – being that of a member of the tribe who had let himself be ritually killed as a kind of willing victim sacrificing himself for the good of the tribe. This communal drinking of the warm blood and eating the gobbets of throbbing flesh, newly killed, of their fellow-tribesmen would revitalise the unity of the group and heal the fractures and tensions within it. As civilisation developed, the human sacrifice was reserved for great occasions as when a group of allied tribes were going to war as described in the Homeric account of the Trojan war, whereas by this time, the flesh ordinarily consumed at the regular rituals was that of the tribal animals whose milk provided the everyday drink of the tribe, whose wool provided their clothing but who were at that stage never eaten except on a religious occasion because their blood (as the result of the drinking of their milk) was identified with the tribe which owned and maintained them.

So far the story is merely conjectural – helped out by analogies and instances from Robertson Smith's remarkable erudition – but the next stage in the story is able to draw some support from the Old Testament. The great dividing line, according to Robertson Smith, is when primitive communism and the matriarchy associated with it gives way to private property and the patriarchal system. Following the lead of Adam Smith, Robertson Smith draws attention to the double-edged ambiguous nature of private property and the specialised system which accompanies it. In improving the standard of living of all sections of the tribe in a material and in some extent an intellectual way (at the cost of introducing a division between rich and poor, nobility and commonality, which didn't exist before), the effect of private property is not, according to Robertson Smith, in all respects bad, as it not merely improves the standard of living but what is more important, fosters a scientific attitude to nature and man's place in it. But on the other hand in regard to the religious side of the life of the now enlarged communities, the effect of the property difference is very damaging as may be seen from the Old Testament. 'Property', says Smith, 'materialises everything it touches', and as a result of the kind of dividing up of functions which attend the wealth-making process the whole meaning of the combination of sacrifice, human or animal, *plus* the ritual meal, which lies at the centre of society in its sacred

phases, becomes misunderstood and totally corrupted in a process that splits the one side off from
the other. On the one hand, the ritual meal part of
the sacred ceremony becomes a sort of good feed of
animal flesh for the rich as well as the priestly case
from which the poor are kept out. On the other hand,
the human sacrifice part becomes institutionalised as
a kind of ceremony of the organised public slaughter
of members of the community, carried out, to
appease the wrath of a godlike monarch in a kind of
sinister stadium for the benefit of the masses who get
a kind of religious thrill from the spectacle. But there
is one redeeming feature of this barbaric civilisation
as described in the Old Testament. Small groups of
people headed by inspired individuals called prophets
keep alive in a reflective clear-headed way some dim
tradition of the manner in which the sacred side of
life had once centred in the participation by the
whole community – not just by the rich – in a ritual
meal, the restorative character of which was not the
good cheer but the fact that the victim eaten had
sacrificed himself in order to restore the group's
feeling of unity by the consumption of his flesh and
blood.

Of course, there is far more to the prophets than a
half-conscious nostalgia for primitive cannibalism. At
the same time as they criticise the barbaric perversion
of primitive religion by the property system by comparison with what happened in the cannibalistic era,

133

they also criticise the cannibalistic era for failing to distinguish between the spiritual side of sacrifice and the material side connected with bloodletting and for emphasising the latter contingent or inessential side by comparison with the essential or spiritual side. Thinking along these lines, the prophets look forward to the human self-sacrifice done to end all human sacrifices, in which a willing victim, by allowing himself be put to death in striking circumstances brings about the religious revolution destined to have irreversible effects. The character of the ceremony is restored to its real meaning as a symbolic communion-meal in which the whole populous participates and not just the rich, while at the same time, the atonement experienced by the participants in the communion is once and for all revealed not as an atonement in the sense of a blood sacrifice to appease a wrathful God, but in the sense of a reidentification with, coupled with a renewal of faith in, a divine plan of a mysterious character which points forward to the end of history and a 'day of judgment', preceded by and prepared by a reintegration into a whole of the scattered and suffering fragments of mankind, especially the Jews. The meaning and purpose of the long and checkered chain of blood sacrifices being at last made clear in the sacrifice to end all sacrifices and the confusions about it dissipated, the communion from now on becomes commemorative, and the bloodshed is abolished from religion.

The denouement of Robertson Smith's story, which he never lived to complete, is sufficiently plain for his readers to spell it out for themselves, however crudely. In due course, Jesus comes on the scene, letting himself be publicly done to death in order to bring to an end the bizarre confusion of matter and spirit which had persisted from time immemorial, and at the same time to promote a renovation of the sacred ritual which would enable all members of the community, irrespective of wealth, to participate in the reanimating effects, public and private, of the religious experience. Blood shedding from now on is to be exclusively confined to the secular side of life which is still characterised – indeed characterised more than ever – by the internecine rivalries of large empires, by the division between rich and poor, by the specialisms that this entails as well as by the science required for understanding and exploiting nature. Nevertheless, the great difference from the Old Testament and pagan days is that the class-divided organisation of society which looks after the secular interests of the group is balanced and checked by the communal participation in the sacred congregatings of society which, regularly punctuating the secular round, looks after the spiritual interests of the group. In this way, the world of civilisation as described by Robertson Smith begins to approximate in its organisation to the ideal embodied in the two kingdoms scheme, in terms of which Andrew

135

Melville sought to interpret the Scottish Reformation, and which Ferrier tried to reformulate in the crisis of the Disruption. Applying the theories of the Scottish Enlightenment to the religious problems which it had itself to some extent neglected, Robertson Smith offers the troubled Scotland of the nineteenth century something it has long sought for but in vain: a vantage point from which to view its ecclesiastical history *sub specie aeterni*.

Taking his cue from J. F. Maclennan, Robertson Smith's speculative reconstruction of history has given new life to the leading ideas of Scotland's other Smith – the four stages of theory and the principle of unintended consequences. Just as the former studies the changes undergone by the exogamy system in response to the movement from a matriarchal scheme without private property, through and by way of a patriarchal scheme with private property towards a subsequent stage in which what looked like commercial societies compete with one another, so too the latter is concerned with expounding the strange transformations which come over the theory and practice of cannibalistic communion, among the Semites and especially the Jews, in the movement from the era of barbaric empire in which religion becomes identical with public slaughter on a mass scale, to the era defined by the pax romana when the religious rituals are subordinated to and made part of the secular state. The experience of living under the

136

brutality of the Moloch-worshipping empire calls into existence the line of prophets who criticise the perversion of the human sacrifice idea as well as the social unfairness from the point of view of vague memories of the cannibalistic communes. So too according to the Robertson Smith theory, the religious revolution in which Christianity comes to the fore arises from the reaction of a Jewish generation brought up on the ideas of their prophets to a situation in which they were expected to conform to the state-religion of the Roman Empire

But while Robertson Smith's speculations are clear enough in so far as they follow out the historical path marked by Maclennan, the question may be, and is in fact raised, as to whether Smith's starting-point – the cannibalistic nature of primitive religion – has the same kind of intelligible foundation in human nature as the premise which Maclennan takes for granted – female infanticide. While female infanticide is (whether true or not in fact) an idea of evident utility from a common sense point of view, the same cannot be said, it is claimed, about the theory that religion is rooted in the bizarre practice of cannibalism. However, without going deeply into the question the difficulty may be cleared, at least in a *prima facie* way, by applying an observation of J.-P. Sartre as to the regular tendency of epistemology to express itself in gastronomic metaphors. To make Sartre's notions on the point fruitful, one must bear in mind a point of view more common in Robertson Smith's time than ours, but defensible even now, which had its origins in classical German philosophy but which was taken over and brilliantly expounded in Scotland by Ferrier, the leading philosopher of the nineteenth century, that in the first place what distinguishes the man from the brute is the self-knowledge or self-consciousness of the former, and secondly, that the self-knowledge in question here isn't a knowledge of one's limitations and peculiarities as an individual compared with other individuals, but rather a knowledge of what one has in common with one's fellows, especially of one's tribe, but in the long run of humanity too. Now the case for considering cannibalism as rooted in human nature becomes clear if we rethink these two contemporary and common ideas of the time in the light of Robertson Smith's distinctive thesis that the primitives don't differentiate properly between spirit and matter, either in their knowledge of the world or their knowledge of themselves. Given this failure to differentiate between the spirit and the flesh, the differentia between man and brute – as constituted by the fact that the members of a human group reaffirm their identity with one another in a manner which brutes do not reaffirm their identity could very well express itself from the point of view of primitives in the ritual cannibalism of which there is no parallel in the animal world. Understood as the material or publicly

138

observable expression of the preoccupation of human beings with self-knowledge in the sense of their repairing the failing or broken sense of identity with their fellow tribesmen, the communal meal in which they eat the flesh and drink the blood of their willing brother would be just as intelligibly rooted in the basic facts of human nature as is Maclennan's female infanticide.

There remains, of course, the important question of the philosophical justifiability of the beliefs presupposed by the evolution of the religious ritual which Robertson Smith describes. Can any meaning, let alone truth, be attached to his considered assertion that supernatural transactions take place – the infusion of grace and so on – as the result of keeping up the sacred ritual? Robertson Smith, indeed, died two or three years after his first series of lectures after a long illness and without being able to do more than give a programme for the second and third series, but the characteristic clarity of the notes he has left both for these and other things, enable us to chart with some confidence his chief lines of explanation and self-justification both in social anthropology and in religious philosophy. As regards the anthropological question, we gather from a letter to his friend Maclennan, whose agnostical point of view he was challenging, that Robertson Smith considered the vital area for a study of the place of supernatural belief in human society was the clash between sorcery

139

and Christianity as it was contemporaneously oc-
curring among the tribesmen of Africa. The evangelical claims about the influx of the supernatural
might, he thinks, be scientifically testable in the
course of a careful study of the effects of Christian
conversion on some Africans.

As regards the philosophical side, Robertson
Smith's brief remarks on the subject of supernatural
influence which he makes in the course of some of his
lectures to the Aberdeen students are, however, much
more illuminating than what he says about African
sorcery. Thoroughly Scottish in his approach to
philosophy, Robertson Smith refers us at once to
David Hume as a kind of intellectual authority.
Robertson Smith thinks Hume's scepticism is valid,
i.e. unanswerable, in its claims as to the limitations in
our knowledge of the human mind, and especially of
other people's minds and the way they communicate
with one another and with us. Because of this
limitation in our knowledge of the way minds work
we cannot pinpoint or isolate a moment of conversion as a datable event as the way in which Loyola
among the Jesuits as well as various Protestant
Evangelists claimed we can. Reflection upon personal
experiences of conversion in oneself or reports of the
kind of thing in others are not helpful in this regard.
But equally, this limitation in our knowledge of the
human mind and its workings does not rule out belief
in transcendent or supernatural influences.

Robertson Smith's treatment of this philosophical crux amounts, as I understand him, to a kind of reaffirmation of Thomas Reid's reply to David Hume's scepticism in regard to religion. Prove to me the existence of other minds, says Reid, and I will prove to you the existence of God. No doubt, Reid's principle does not justify religious beliefs and alleged communications from above in the sense of proving them true, but it does justify them by proving them meaningful and in that sense credible. But, Robertson Smith himself asks in this connection, what more can we do? In an age of science, Robertson Smith says, theology inevitably turns into apologetics, that is the defence of the meaningfulness of belief. The interpretation of the Bible as the story of the relation of cannibalism to Christianity seems in this sense to be compatible with Robertson Smith's claim that he is a follower of Calvin.

Ranking in intellectual quality with some of the best things produced by the historiographical speculations of the Scottish Enlightenment and to a certain extent completing the programme of the Enlightenment by applying its favourite method of research to a field which Ferguson and company had avoided for fear of David Hume, that is the field of religion, Robertson Smith's *Religion of the Semites* and his *Family and Kinship in Arabia* make their quality clear to us by virtue of the series of powerful repercussions which they produced through the West at the time and which in one form or another have continued to the present day. Engels, it would appear, disliked them very much. Reading between the lines of the long diatribe against Maclennan in his introduction to the fourth edition of *The Origin of the Family* one feels that Engels' real target is the growing prestige of Robertson Smith's *Religion of The Semites* which had just been published some eighteen months before, and whose conclusions Engels himself was making use of in an article published in 1896 on the social significance of early Christianity.

However, if Marxists naturally enough shied away from Robertson Smith, others of the rising stars in the intellectual firmament were differently disposed. Freud, for example, acknowledges his debt to both Robertson Smith's books – the one on religion as well as the one on the family – although he plays down the cannibalism bit which is obviously too much even for Freud. Durkheim in France, though also playing down the human sacrifice theme, makes no secret of how much, not only his view of the social foundations of religion, but also his general programme for sociology, owes to his reading of Robertson Smith. In the English-speaking world, especially at Oxford and Cambridge, Robertson Smith's writings also made a powerful impact although their meaning was to some extent obscured and weakened by the people who took them up. The pupil of Smith's last years – Sir

James Frazer (as he became) – popularised the Robertson Smith view of religion, perverting it in the process not only by playing up the cannibalism in the interests of an aesthetic *frisson* but also by suppressing the 'unintended consequences' aspect of the theory in the interests of replacing Robertson Smith's affirmation of a sceptically based faith with superficial positivism.

Throughout the West, then, Robertson Smith's theories made and still make a lasting mark but in Scotland itself things have turned out very differently. What has kept his memory alive here is his central role in the dramatic decade of church troubles in which the religious passions of the nation rose to the final crescendo of a climax, not the Aberdeen lectures on *The Religion of the Semites* which, delivered five or six years after his extrusion from his Chair, constituted in effect his considered comments on the Scottish struggles about religious principle, but which, though interesting for the rest of the world have hardly interested the Scots at all.

Donald Carswell,[6] in his remarkable essay, and James Bulloch[7] in his stimulating chapter, bring out Robertson Smith's significance for Scotland in terms of the two-facedness of Principal Rainy, of the plotting of Dr Begg and Kennedy of Dingwall and the Free Church lobby, of the queue at 6 a.m. on the May morning to hear the fourteen-hour-long debate on Deuteronomy which resulted in Robertson Smith's unexpected acquittal, and finally of the equally unexpected triumph of his enemies a few weeks later as the result of the belated publication of an article sent to the press years before and now forgotten on the fatal topic of totemism in the Old Testament. But at the same time these essayists and historians who – like Carswell – display such nerve and wit in bringing out the significance of the Robertson Smith case as a landmark in the collapse of intellectual and moral standards in Scotland, entirely fail to bring out the significance of Robertson Smith in the very different sense of showing how the masterpiece he produced on the nature of religion – in addition to serving as his self-justification in the face of prejudice – magnificently transcends the whole squalid episode and incidentally, by a kind of unintended consequence, vindicates and redeems the fifty years of religious strife which made Scotland and the Scottish people a byword through the West for social irresponsibility and sectarian vindictiveness. As happens also in the case of Ferrier and of J. F. Maclennan, the Scots pay attention only to the humiliating side of their history: the former was excluded from the philosophical Chairs in the metropolis of Edinburgh as the result of the intrigues of the Free Church lobby, on account of the allegedly un-Scottish nature of his ideas, the failure of the latter's practice as an advocate and the freezing of him out of Edinburgh again was because of the supposed un-Scottish tendency of his speculations about the matriarchy and female infanticide. Occupied only with the shortcomings of the country, Scottish opinion has far too little consciousness of the exhilarating fact that the downfall of Ferrier and of Maclennan and of Smith was due to their very success in giving a new lease of life to the standards of the Scottish Enlightenment, both in regard to the nature of human knowledge and in regard to the speculative reconstruction of early history. Leaving it to other countries, and not least England, to appreciate the intellectual achievements of men like this, the Scots perversely preoccupy themselves only with the side of their nineteenth-century history which shows their country to have been a failure.

Notes

1. Jones and Muirhead, *The Life of Edward Caird*, p. 270.
2. It was equally familiar in Edinburgh. Flint's book *Socialism* (1891) contains a powerful criticism of the argument of *Das Kapital*, based on lectures to workers of the Edinburgh of the 1880s.
3. S. S. Laurie's *Scotus Novanticus* and the trilogy by Andrew Seth (Pringle-Pattison): *Scottish Philosophy, Hegelianism and Personality*, and *Realism*.
4. E. Husserl, *Crisis of European Sciences*, Evanston, 1970, pp. 21-69.
5. In the National Library of Scotland.
6. D. Carswell, *Brother Scots*, London 1927, pp. 54-119.
7. A. L. Drummond and James Bulloch, *The Church in late-Victorian Scotland*, Edinburgh, 1978, pp. 40-79.